Identity Development of Diverse Populations: Implications for Teaching and Administration in Higher Education

Vasti Torres, Mary F. Howard-Hamilton, Diane L. Cooper

ASHE-ERIC Higher Education Report: Volume 29, Number 6
Adrianna J. Kezar, Series Editor

Prepared and published by

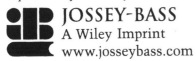

JOSSEY-BASS
A Wiley Imprint
www.josseybass.com

In cooperation with

ERIC Clearinghouse on Higher Education
The George Washington University
URL: www.eriche.org

Association for the Study
of Higher Education
URL: www.tiger.coe.missouri.edu/~ashe

Graduate School of Education and Human Development
The George Washington University
URL: www.gwu.edu

Identity Development of Diverse Populations: Implications for Teaching and Administration in Higher Education
Vasti Torres, Mary F. Howard-Hamilton, Diane L. Cooper
ASHE-ERIC Higher Education Report: Volume 29, Number 6
Adrianna J. Kezar, Series Editor

This publication was prepared partially with funding from the Office of Educational Research and Improvement, U.S. Department of Education, under contract no. ED-99-00-0036. The opinions expressed in this report do not necessarily reflect the positions or policies of OERI or the Department.

ISSN 0884-0040   electronic ISSN 1536-0709   ISBN 0-7879-6351-8

The ASHE-ERIC Higher Education Report is part of the Jossey-Bass Higher and Adult Education Series and is published six times a year by Wiley Subscription Services, Inc., A Wiley Company, at Jossey-Bass, 989 Market Street, San Francisco, California 94103-1741.

For subscription information, see the Back Issue/Subscription Order Form in the back of this journal.

CALL FOR PROPOSALS: Prospective authors are strongly encouraged to contact Adrianna Kezar at the University of Southern California, Waite Phillips Hall 703C, Los Angeles, CA 90089, or kezar@usc.edu. See "About the ASHE-ERIC Higher Education Report Series" in the back of this volume.

Visit the Jossey-Bass Web site at **www.josseybass.com.**

Executive Summary

The idea for this monograph came from discussions among graduate faculty about how to deal with the issues of race, ethnicity, and other controversial issues in the classroom and around campus. Each of us could tell numerous stories about the mishandling of issues by faculty and administrators that focused on a misunderstood student from a different race, ethnicity, or social group other than the majority. The result of the misunderstanding can sometimes result in a campus conflict where others are involved without understanding the issues at hand. And it happens in higher education much more often than we care to admit.

Why Is a Discussion of Ethnic Identity Development Necessary?

The number of racially and ethnically diverse students on our college campuses has profoundly increased. What is more significant is the diversity within these groups. Students are becoming connected with their "homeland" and expressing this connection through their racial and ethnic identity. Concomitantly, the number is growing of biracial and multiracial students on campus whose identities blend and intersect with several cultures and contexts. The expansion and complexity of these groups necessitate a review of the current theories written for adolescent and college student populations. Reexamining foundational identity theories and expounding on the theories that address racial identity development can provide faculty and administrators with the ability to make the appropriate application for students who attend higher education institutions.

What often is not recognized is that demographic shifts are also occurring within the faculty and administrative ranks. Collegial interactions are changing with the influx of more women, people of color, and persons from other cultural backgrounds interacting with majority group members. Interactions in the classroom are changing as a result of students who have not had any significant contact or communication with racially or ethnically diverse professionals, which may create problems in the classroom and campus community. Everyone needs to be held accountable for enhancing his or her own level of multicultural competence and sensitivity to diverse groups.

Why Is This Information So Necessary for Higher Education Practice?

Hoare (1994) notes that "there is a strong correlation between the extent to which we understand our own conscious and unconscious biases and our abilities to unimposingly hear and care about those who do not share our culturally grounded views" (pp. 37–38). Our practice has not always been in sync with the changing populations on our college campuses. For us to hear and care, we need to challenge our presupposed ideas, biases, and prejudices about how we teach, practice, and interact with our students and colleagues.

A good example of the changing landscape is how predominantly white institutions may reflect the views and policies that are alienating to students from diverse populations. This monograph is written to challenge the traditional paradigms and recognize new voices that should be part of the construction of new, more inclusive policies and practices.

This monograph focuses on educating faculty and administrators about the developmental issues faced by students from different racial, ethnic, or social groups as they attempt to define themselves during the college years. By presenting the existing research and theories on the development of identity and the particular effects of this process on diverse students, we hope to foster greater understanding and dialogue. Attitudes about differences are influenced by how students make meaning of their own race and ethnicity, making it critical that all those who work on a college campus also understand how this identity is developed.

How Can Our Practice Become More Intentional Around Ethic Identity Development?

As diversity came to the forefront in the 1970s, colleges and universities rushed to create courses in African American studies, Chicano studies, and women's studies, to name a few. Today, an infusion process is necessary rather than adding on to the curriculum. Faculty need to understand they have "new learners" in their classrooms and design assignments that include everyone and allow for students to learn and understand divergent points of views. Student affairs professionals also need to be more intentional in their programming, developing new and inclusive policies, mission statements, and learning goals that also reflect this new way of valuing diversity. Perhaps the baseline for new practice should be the question "Have I included everyone in the activities, programs, or syllabus I just created?"

We acknowledge that this monograph will make some readers uncomfortable, yet we view this discomfort as part of the process of creating a positive environment for all. Each faculty member and administrator must understand how he or she as an individual and as a member of the institution influences the success or failure of those who are not from the majority white culture. It is only when this discomfort is dealt with that higher education can truly say, "we value diversity."

Contents

Foreword — ix

Why Should Higher Education Be Concerned with the Identity Development of Diverse Students? — 1

Development of Identity — 2

Definitions — 6

Organization — 8

Theoretical Frameworks of Identity Development Theory: Foundational Theories — 9

Foundational Theories of Identity Development — 9

Evaluation of Foundational Theories — 14

Dominant Cultures, Oppression, and Other Societal Issues Affecting the Identity Development of Diverse Populations — 17

Cultural and Societal Issues That Impact Identity Development — 18

Theory of Oppression — 19

The Social Oppression Matrix — 21

Social Identity Development Theory — 23

How Oppression Impacts Privileged Groups — 25

White Identity Theories — 27

Conclusion — 31

**Theoretical Frameworks of Diverse Identity Development
Theories: A View Through a Different Lens**   **33**

Multigroup Ethnic and Racial Identity Models   33

Racial and Ethnic Identity Theories Pertaining to African
    American Students   39

Racial and Ethnic Identity Theories Pertaining to Native
    American Students   49

Acculturation to the Majority Culture   52

Racial and Ethnic Identity Theories Pertaining to Latino
    and Latina Students   53

Racial and Ethnic Identity Theories Pertaining to Asian
    American Students   59

Multiracial Identity   64

Conclusion   66

**Multiple Identities: Acknowledging the
Interrelationship Among Roles**   **67**

Integrating Multiple Layers of Identity Development   69

Sexual Orientation Identity Formation   73

Women and Gender Identity   76

Implications   78

Integration of Identity Development Theory into Practice   **79**

Campus Culture   80

Implications for Administrators   82

Implications for Faculty Members   86

Conclusions and Future Implications   99

**Appendix A. Case Study: Defining Academic
Diversity at Reflective College**   **101**

Considerations in Addressing This Issue   **103**

References   **107**

Index   **119**

Foreword

Over the past decade, several ASHE-ERIC monographs have examined ways to increase the diversity of students and faculty, to retain students from diverse backgrounds, and to create more inclusive campus environments. Most works have focused on sociological, policy, or organizational frameworks to understand ways to reorganize and reexamine our institutional cultures. A gap in our knowledge about how to create a more inclusive environment has been the identity development of individuals that make up our campus communities. Vasti Torres, Mary F. Howard-Hamilton, and Diane L. Cooper help fill this gap in this new monograph, *Identity Development of Diverse Populations: Implications for Teaching and Administration in Higher Education.* It focuses on educating faculty and administrators about the developmental issues faced by students from different racial, ethnic, or other social groups as they attempt to define themselves during the college years and the ways this information can enhance campus classrooms, programs, and policies. Although a growing body of work is available on how various racial, ethnic, gender, and other social groups develop their identity, there has been limited synthesis or application of this literature to the practice of professionals in higher education. The authors' recommendations are grounded in experience as educational administrators, and each has a solid record of scholarship in identity development.

Several aspects make this monograph a particularly strong synthesis of the literature. First, it is among the first monographs to bring together specific group identity (African American, for example), multiracial and multigroup, and multi-identity models (combining race, gender, and sexual orientation, for example). Identity has often been looked at in ways that are too facile. This monograph portrays a complex portrait of identity development that will surely enhance the understanding of campus faculty and administrators. A second strength is the presentation of oppression theories. Too often, discussions of differences in identity development do not address the inequitable power relations that exist and shape and frame our experiences. This monograph does not shy away from presenting what can be challenging material for those with privilege, often the campus leaders the monograph is aimed at engaging in dialogue. A third strength is the enumeration of detailed and thoughtful implications for changing campus cultures by designing institutional assessments, involving diverse persons in decision making, examining cultural artifacts, understanding how culture influences classrooms, and introducing new teaching strategies.

This monograph could not be published at a more opportune time as we reflect on the fifty-year anniversary of *Brown* v. *Board of Education* (in 2004). I hope that this anniversary will serve as a time for campuses to reflect on the way they have changed (or stayed the same) in terms of becoming more inclusive environments. As we continue to evolve as a multiracial, multiethnic, and multiidentity society, we need more tools to continue to move forward. I hope readers will use the theories synthesized by and recommendations offered by the authors to enhance institutional performance and equity, an unfinished agenda.

Adrianna J. Kezar
Series Editor

Why Should Higher Education Be Concerned with the Identity Development of Diverse Students?

A MAJOR GOAL OF HIGHER EDUCATION is to be a marketplace of ideas. This goal is valued and often referred to when people discuss controversial issues. What is not often discussed is the response most people have when they have strongly opposing beliefs about important issues. Most people have one of two responses to disagreements: (1) engage in a dialogue with the aim of better understanding the other side so as to convince them to change their mind, and (2) intentionally avoid the individual and, when encounters are forced, actively avoid the controversial issue (Miller and Prentice, 1999). Often when individuals belong to different racial, ethnic, gender, social class, sexual orientation, or other social groups, the differences among the groups become the explanation for the disagreement. A possible outcome of this explanation is that with time, the differences can become "more unbridgeable when they occur between members of different groups than between members of the same group" (Miller and Prentice, 1999, p. 215). This potential communication gap can happen when faculty and administrators in higher education attempt a dialogue with students from various racial, ethnic, or social groups without having knowledge about the differences and similarities in the identity development of individuals within the groups as well as how one's own social group identity impacts that interaction. Institutions of higher education are not necessarily equipped to deal with the emotional conflict that can occur when dealing with issues of race and ethnicity (Smith, 1996).

A study by Hurtado (1996) found that one in four students at four-year colleges perceived "considerable racial conflict" on the campus (p. 492). Only 12 percent of students at four-year colleges thought racial discrimination was no longer a problem in the United States (Hurtado, 1996). These data illustrate that conflict over race or ethnicity continues to be an issue on campus and will continue to be as the controversy about affirmative action continues (Schmidt, 2003; Selingo, 2003). Dialogue among people from diverse backgrounds is a critical element of the marketplace of ideas, yet sometimes these conversations are strained, difficult, and painful for one or both sides. The fear of being misunderstood paralyzes the conversations, making the dialogue even more difficult (Tatum, 1996).

The best way to improve intergroup interactions is to provide information that can educate individuals, particularly information about the variety of opinions, behaviors, and perceptions of any particular group. "Through education, it is possible to teach people that not all the differences they experience with members of other categories [social groups] are category differences" (Miller and Prentice, 1999, p. 234). This monograph is the first step in educating oneself about students from different racial, ethnic, or social groups as they attempt to define themselves during the college years. Because not all students are alike, it is important that we understand their identity development process rather than make overgeneralized statements about group membership. Attitudes about differences are influenced by how students make meaning of their own race and ethnicity. By understanding the similarities and differences in the identity development process of diverse groups of college students, faculty and administrators will be better able to dialogue about those differences.

> **Because not all students are alike, it is important that we understand their identity development process rather than make overgeneralized statements about group membership.**

Development of Identity

The majority of individuals who have attended college note how much they changed during this period of their lives. From this intuitive sense of development, or change, which occurs during late adolescence, individuals create a sense of self that usually feels more grounded and stable. Student development theory emerged from investigating these changes and the sense of self that develops as a result of the changes. A central notion of student development has always been the idea that the college years are critical for the development of identity. Erikson (1968) saw the late adolescent years as a time of conflict between identity and identity diffusion. It is the resolution of this conflict that influences how identity develops. Chickering and Reisser (1993) expanded on the process of resolving conflict with the notion of identity development through seven vectors that students work on mastering during their time in college. The belief that students' sense of identity is developed during the college years is widely accepted; what has not received as much attention is the influence of race, ethnicity, other social categories, or the interrelationship of multiple identities on that development during the college years.

Pascarella and Terenzini (1991) noted the "absence of studies dealing with identity development among Black (or other minority) students" (p. 166). The absence of this type of research has forced faculty and administrators to apply identity development theories that were formed from studies of white students (often not including women) to all students regardless of gender, race, ethnicity, or other differences. The application of these theories to students from very different racial or ethnic backgrounds can cause misunderstandings and miscommunications. The desire to intentionally influence positive learning and development requires those working in higher education to understand what conflicts students must resolve to develop their sense of self and in turn how we can assist them in resolving those conflicts.

Clear evidence suggests that the developmental process for racially and ethnically diverse students is "more than dichotomous to one group . . . than another. Moreover, the consequences or outcomes of the developmental process may have implications for the individual's level of adjustment as well as for the quality of the interactions in which she or he engages and for the environment . . . generally" (Helms, 1994, p. 306). The desire to help students adjust positively to the college environment requires faculty and administrators to be familiar with the developmental issues facing these diverse students.

The study of racial and ethnic identity spans several disciplines. Anthropologists tend to describe theories about race and ethnicity as discussions of classifications and boundary maintenance (Banks, 1996), while sociologists' theories of race are "defined by situations where phenotypically dissimilar groups are in some sort of long-term unequal power and/or economic relationship and where the dominant group justifies its position through some kind of legitimating ideology" (p. 54). This monograph does not attempt to define the characteristics of a racial, ethnic, or social group. Rather, it focuses on understanding the experiences of those who come from a different race, ethnic, or social group than the dominant group in the United States. This approach is in congruence with a sociological approach, yet much of the work that has been done on the actual identity development process has been conducted from a psychosocial perspective. In deciding what should be included in this monograph, the authors chose to focus on research conducted specifically on individuals in the early adult years or specifically on college students.

The authors of this monograph have used a broad definition of diversity that includes race, ethnicity, and multiple identities that encompass gender and sexual orientation. The approach presented in this monograph is based on the idea that a person must recognize one's own culture before truly understanding another person's culture. To accomplish this aim, the authors look at societal issues involving issues of race and ethnicity as well as examine how these societal issues have influenced the development of white people's cultural identity. The fact that the dominant group of faculty and administrators in higher education continues to be white men (72.1 percent) or white women (17.3 percent) (Harvey, 2001) makes the inclusion of white identity theory a necessity. It is the authors' desire that this monograph promote reflection, dialogue, and understanding for both dominant and nonsubordinate groups.

Dominant groups (usually identified as whites in the United States) "set the parameters within which subordinates operate. The dominant group holds the power and the authority in society relative to the subordinates and determines how that power and authority may be acceptably used" (Tatum, 1997, p. 23). History has illustrated the relationship between the dominant and subordinates as often based on the targeted group's (subordinates') being "labeled as defective or substandard" (p. 23). For example, the dominant group historically has characterized women (the subordinate group) as less emotionally stable than men. Certain dominant group members historically have believed that African Americans are less intelligent than whites (Tatum, 1997). The relationship between dominant and subordinate groups, such as minorities, requires that any discussion of identity include the influence of these stereotypes on the subordinate group. The influence of this phenomenon can best be understood through a discussion of oppression and how racial and ethnic minority identities are influenced by these stereotypes. Research has shown that the existence of a negative stereotype about a group to which one belongs can result in negative performance, referred to as *stereotype threat* (Steele and Aronson, 1995). In situations where the stereotype may be applicable (like stereotypes of lower performance than whites on academic tests), "one is at risk of confirming it [the stereotype] as a self-characterization, both to one's self and to others who know the stereotype" (p. 808). In studies looking at stereotype threat, two groups of students were given tests, with each group given difference information. When race was given as a reason for poor performance, students of that race performed lower than white students. When race was not given as a reason for poor performance, students of that race did as well as white students (Steele and Aronson, 1995). These studies illustrate the power of the words we speak; we need to be aware of how faculty and administrators influence the performance of racially and ethnically diverse students. This power makes it necessary for all faculty and administrators to understand how their behavior can be interpreted and how they can influence the success of diverse students. The knowledge of how identity develops for these diverse groups can help further the understanding needed to help students succeed. The emphasis in this country on "racial markers as preliminary credentials for access to reward or punishment" makes racial membership a core element of identity development in the United States (Helms, 1994, p. 286).

As a result of societal influences, identity models for diverse populations emphasize experiences with oppression and those who are considered "minority." This minority status comes with historical connotations and societal norms that obligate us to also look at the consequences of stereotypes and in turn oppression (Birman, 1994).

The inclusion of white identity theories, which focus on the perception and reaction to other racial groups, can assist in the understanding needed to change society. The authors chose to include white identity development, because the majority of faculty and staff in higher education continues to be white, making whites the dominant group (Harvey, 2001), and because these theories set the stage for the type of personal development that is needed to deal with other races, cultures, and lifestyles. To change the campus environment, all members of the college community must engage in understanding differences and accepting their own roles in the present campus culture.

The most distinguishable difference between identity development theories based on majority white populations and those from racial, ethnic, or other socially subordinate groups is the presence of oppression and how individuals cope with it. By looking at the consequences of oppression, we hope to illustrate how historical context and societal views have impacted and continue to influence how diverse students adapt in the college environment.

Definitions

Before we can begin to introduce theories and models, it is important that the reader understand the nuances of different terms used to describe diverse populations.

- *Race* deals with how humankind socially categorizes the hereditary traits of different groups of people, thus creating socially defined differences. These traits are biologically visible and deal mainly with skin color and physical differences. Centuries of racial mixing have made it difficult to "unequivocally differentiate one so-called racial group from another" (Helms, 1994, p. 295).
- *Ethnicity* is a social identity based on a person's historical nationality or tribal group. For this reason, any one racial group comprises many ethnicities (Helms, 1994). In the context of this monograph, this social identity is based on membership in a segment, or social group, of a larger society that does not share the same culture (Yinger, 1994).
- *Culture* should be considered from a broad level (macroculture) and a subsidiary level. On a broad level, culture provides individuals with an

identity and value orientation that represents a society (such as a country). This broad level can contain subsidiary cultures that focus on customs, values, traditions, and histories from different broad cultures (such as Mexican culture within the broad U.S. culture) (Helms, 1994).

- *Acculturation* is the process that occurs when an individual is placed in a culture different from the one he or she previously lived in. Though early models of acculturation focused on the loss of one culture to gain the new culture, more recent research has proved that loss and negative interactions are not a requirement in this process and that individuals learn to adapt without loss of their culture of origin (Garza and Gallegos, 1995).
- *Social group* is used to describe membership in a socially defined segment of the population that is not the majority, including membership groups according to gender, social class, or sexual orientation.

It is our goal to challenge, inspire, and promote dialogue through this monograph. A college student's identity development is a complex and individual process based on choices that bring congruence between old and new learned beliefs. The complexity of this process makes it difficult to create concrete road maps for how to deal with students undergoing the process of solidifying their identity. Instead, theories help frame and explain aspects of the process. We do not claim to have concrete responses; we hope only to inform practice and provide educators with more tools to consider in their daily interactions with students. If higher education is sincere about creating positive learning environments for all students, then each person who works with diverse populations must also value these diverse developmental issues. The marketplace of ideas can be more fruitful when constructive, informed dialogue is expected and valued on the college campus.

If higher education is sincere about creating positive learning environments for all students, then each person who works with diverse populations must also value these diverse developmental issues.

Organization

The monograph begins with a discussion of why those in higher education should be concerned about the identity development of diverse populations. It is followed by a discussion of foundational identity theories that provide the groundwork for understand identity. Because foundational theories do not address the societal issues that influence how we see race, ethnicity, and other social groups in the United States, the following chapter is devoted to the influence of oppression on minority students. Part of that chapter also focuses on white identity theories that conceptualize white people's perception and reaction to other racial groups.

Once the foundational concept of societal views and oppression has been covered, existing theoretical frameworks are presented to illustrate the development of various racial and ethnic groups in the United States as well as theories dealing with the concept of multiple identities. The final chapter integrates the research presented to illustrate the implications for practice and recommendations for the future. It is the authors' hope that readers view this discussion as a starting point for investigating the diversity of identity development theories and use it as a springboard for deeper investigation.

Theoretical Frameworks of Identity Development Theory: Foundational Theories

THE STUDY OF IDENTITY DEVELOPMENT, compared with other constructs, is a fairly recent phenomenon, and each theorist has built on the previous theories. These theories, although somewhat simplistic and based on the dominant culture in their development and presentation, are discussed here to provide a frame of reference for considering the more complex concepts of ethnic and multiple identity development presented later in this monograph. This chapter focuses on the early theories of identity development and then reviews research on these theories.

Foundational Theories of Identity Development

Foundational theories about identity are by nature broad in their scope. This section includes short summaries of the work of Erikson, Marcia, Josselson, and Chickering and Reisser, all of which provide the background necessary to understand later research on identity.

Erikson

Erikson's work (1964) is usually the theory mentioned at the onset of examining general bodies of research related to identity development. Erikson defined identity as "the ability to experience one's self as something that has continuity and sameness, and to act accordingly" (1964, p. 42). Conversely, Erikson also asserted that in addition to gaining a sense of who we are, our identities are formed by the process of discovering who we are *not* (Erikson, 1964). These components of his model have served as a basis for numerous identity models to follow (see, for example, Ivey, Ivey, and Simek-Morgan, 1993). Although Erikson's theory serves as a foundation, some would argue, however, that his theory alone does not explain aspects of racial and ethnic development (Chestang, 1984; Foster and Perry, 1982).

Central to this theory is the development of ego (that part of the personality that brings order out of our experiences). Our identity is the outward expression of our ego or who we really are. Erikson believed that the ego emerged part by part, as if like a plan (following developmental stages).

The process of developing identity involves a linear process in which individuals develop ego "strengths" to successfully complete a developmental task (or stage) to move to the next task. Stages of development require a resolution of prior stage tasks before the stage is mastered.

At the theory's root is the concept of *ego epigenesis,* or the belief that a planned sequence of biological and psychosocial phases exists. Three domains of ego epigenesis require examination of a person's (1) physical stage, (2) encounter with society and the social roles played, and (3) internal ordering of those experiences (ego functioning). "He proposed that membership identities, including social class, culture, and national affiliation, provided people with the collective power to create their own environment" (Ivey, Ivey, and Simek-Morgan, 1993, p. 76). Erikson was one of the earliest theorists to consider the role of environment in creating a sense of self, an important factor in considering the ethnic identity theories and models discussed later in this text.

Erikson's theory has eight psychosocial stages, with movement from one stage to the next creating a change in our identity. Stages have a cumulative relationship or influence on each other stage. Two polarized attributes are part of each stage (for example, trust versus mistrust). One can emerge from a stage feeling positive about his or her personal and social capacities or with a sense of self that may become debilitating later in life. Erikson calls them *nuclear conflicts* or a time when we vacillate between these contradictory views of ourselves. Eventually individuals reach a crisis point or a time when a decision will be made. Crisis is not a major trauma but a time to take one road or another. If we take the positive view of the stage, we develop *ego strengths,* which Erikson calls "virtues." These virtues add up over time and assist us later in life. Development takes place through "dissonance." The right amount of tension is needed to produce change. The range of optimal dissonance can vary depending on the quality of challenge and support (Sanford, 1962) available in the environment. The focus of most college student development theories is on the stage identity versus identity confusion that occurs in late adolescence. Because stabilizing identity is the focal developmental task of young adults, it is natural that this stage be the launching point of identity development among college students (Chickering and Reisser, 1993).

Marcia

James Marcia (1966), building on Erikson's theory, explored the development of identity along two dimensions; (1) awareness of an identity crisis that must be explored and resolved, and (2) making a commitment to the identity after a period of exploring various ways of being. The tabular relationship of these two dimensions to each other results in four quadrants that explain the constructs of this theory (see Table 1). The emphasis of this theory is on the process through which identity is developed; identity is not necessarily viewed as occurring in stages. It assumes that commitments may be manifest even though we cannot see the identity structure. It also assumes that identity can exist even though we do not see the commitments we have made.

A *foreclosed* individual has not experienced a crisis of identity but nevertheless has made a commitment to an identity. These individuals do not separate from their family and are not influenced by friends, classroom material, or cocurricular experiences. They tend to hold on to traditional social or family norms without questioning them.

TABLE 1
Marcia's Identity Development Model

| | | Commitment? | |
		YES	NO
Exploration or	YES	Identity Achievement	Diffusion
Crisis?	NO	Moratorium	Foreclosure

Those individuals with a *diffused* identity have neither committed to an identity nor experienced a crisis related to identity development. Typically, it is expected that the individual has experienced both the dimensions by the time he or she has completed college. Those individuals who have experienced some type of identity crisis that did not result in further exploration and identity commitment are said to be in identity *moratorium*. For these individuals, a conscious search is under way, but not all the alternatives have been understood or evaluated. This situation can result in an unstable time when the individual is trying out different identities, experimenting with various ways of being, or observing others they wish to emulate. Finally, when a person has experienced a crisis that resulted in further exploration and commitment to an identity, Marcia would say this person is now *identity achieved*. In this case, the crises have been endured and meaningful commitments have been independently made.

Josselson

Through extensive interviews during research on women's identity development (1987), Josselson noted that women could be characterized in similar ways. Josselson's work gives us another lens through which to view the process of identity development, specifically for women. Using Marcia's model as a framework, Josselson found four statuses assumed by women:

- *Foreclosures*—Purveyors of Heritage. These women were strongly committed but had not explored much on their own. These women highly valued following family traditions and meeting familial expectations. They pursued their goals with a single-minded determination, without doubt or hesitation.
- *Identity Achievers*—Pavers of the Way—formed separate, distinct identities from their childhood. They took pride in themselves and believed their occupations to be an expression of themselves.
- *Moratoriums*—Daughters of Crisis—were women who were always searching and experimenting, seeking an "idealized perfection" (Evans, Forney, and Guido-DiBrito, 1998, p. 61) and seeming always to need more time to sort through things.

- *Identity Diffusions*—Lost–Sometimes Found women were lowest in ego development, had the most difficulty establishing relationships, had high anxiety, and tended to withdraw from situations. These women also experienced feelings of powerlessness.

Chickering and Reisser

Many college student development theorists based their work on Erikson; preeminent among them is Arthur Chickering. The framework for Chickering's theory of education and identity includes seven vectors or developmental tasks (see Chickering, 1969; Chickering and Reisser, 1993). Typically, traditional-aged college students explore the first three vectors in their first few years of college, while upperclass students wrestle with vectors four, five, and possibly six. Individuals continue to work through the later vectors throughout their life and may revisit issues within a vector as they develop.

According to Chickering and Reisser (1993), colleges that help students perform at their ability and readiness level lay the foundation for the first vector, *developing competence,* which includes intellectual social, and physical competence. Personal achievements, even those involving pre-college reading and writing or extracurricular activities, are more likely to facilitate an increase in students' competence than are academic credits earned toward graduation. Feelings of competence come from confidence in one's ability to cope with what comes and to achieve desired goals. The second vector, *managing emotions,* is where individuals learn to direct strong emotions in appropriate channels. Dealing with fear, anger, depression, and possibly dysfunctional sexual or romantic attractions can be commonplace for individuals in this vector. In the third vector, *moving through autonomy to interdependence,* self-sufficiency is the key in this focus on emotional and instrumental interdependence. Dealing with family members and maintaining connections to significant others while becoming autonomous are also important tasks related to this vector.

> **Feelings of competence come from confidence in one's ability to cope with what comes and to achieve desired goals.**

The fourth vector is *developing mature interpersonal relationships,* or the ability to create intimacy with another person as well as develop tolerance and an appreciation for others' differences. The fifth vector is *establishing identity;* identity includes a positive sense of self with respect to body, gender, and sexual orientation, for example. Stability and integration of all aspects of self are critical. According to Chickering, students cannot truly master this vector until they have mastered the previous four vectors.

In the sixth vector, *developing purpose,* the individual focuses on vocational plans, personal interests, and being intentional and goal oriented about family. Students may begin to explore this vector while still in college, but these issues will continue to be present throughout their lifetime. Issues of the seventh vector, *developing integrity,* will also be present throughout one's life. Developing congruence between beliefs and actions and humanizing and personalizing values are central issues of this vector.

Chickering and Reisser's work provides a comprehensive, easy-to-understand model of how college students change psychosocially. Although the model is often applied to everyone, Reisser (1995) notes that more research is needed on its applicability to various student subpopulations (based on race, sexual orientation, ethnicity, and gender). Even traditionally used measures of the model's constructs have clearly shown differences based on gender and race (Winston, Miller, and Cooper, 1999). As Evans, Forney, and Guido-DiBrito (1998) note, "It may not be possible to develop a theory that is totally valid for everyone" (p. 51). In fact, many researchers working since the early 1970s began to see identity through the lens of "difference." For this reason, theorists have attempted to look at diverse student populations through a slightly different lens that expands the notions of the earlier theorist.

Evaluation of Foundational Theories

More recently, Arnett (2000) has questioned Erikson's notion of identity development, arguing that we need to consider "emerging adulthood" as more characteristic of the traditional 18- to 24-year-old period of life in industrialized nations. "Emerging adults tend to have a wider scope of possible activities than persons in other age periods because they are less likely to be constrained by role requirements" (p. 471). This period of time seems to be tied to the postponement of traditional adult roles of worker, parent, or spouse and thus readily applies to traditional undergraduate students. Activities often associated with identity development during college, such as the exploration of self and role testing, are characteristics of emerging adulthood. The exploration of racial identity development in the context of this period needs to be further examined, and Arnett makes a strong case for the need to regard the role of cultural influences during this time period.

Other research studies have considered traditional theories and their application to diverse populations. Taub and McEwen (1992) found that African American "women may experience developmental pulls in different directions by their psychosocial development of autonomy and interpersonal relationships on the one hand and their racial identity development on the other hand" (p. 444). This study suggests that there are two separate and different processes of development occurring for African American college women—racial identity development and psychosocial development. One of the factors considered in explaining the results of this study was that the environment at predominantly white colleges can be counterproductive to the development of African American students and thus postpone or delay their development. Instead, black students must focus their energies of survival behaviors such as developing intellectual competence and dealing with the social isolation found at predominantly white institutions (Taub and McEwen, 1992).

To incorporate African American students into the psychosocial theories, McEwen, Roper, Bryant, and Langa (1990) suggested that nine factors must be considered in the research: (1) developing ethnic and racial identity, (2) interacting with the dominant culture, (3) developing cultural aesthetics and awareness, (4) developing integrity, (5) developing interdependence, (6) fulfilling affiliation needs, (7) surviving intellectually, (8) developing spirituality, and (9) developing social responsibility. These factors illustrate the importance of viewing the racial

The environment at predominantly white colleges can be counterproductive to the development of African American students and thus postpone or delay their development.

development of African American students along with their social and cognitive development.

Though these studies have focused primarily on African Americans, they illustrate that foundational theories do not encompass the developmental tasks of diverse student populations. They also illustrate that the environment at predominantly white institutions is not the same for all students. These differences focus on the societal traditions involved in oppressing those who are different. The fact that the foundational theories are developed on the values and assumptions of European Americans makes simple revisions inappropriate. Instead, it seems more appropriate to create new theories than to revise the foundational ones (McEwen, Roper, Bryant, and Langa, 1990).

This overview of identity development theories lays the groundwork for the consideration of models that are focused on racial and ethnic identity development. The important life question—"Who am I?"—is only partially addressed in the previously discussed theories. This question takes on different orientations for those individuals in the nondominant culture. Many additional considerations must be explored and understood to fully appreciate the difficulty of developing an identity while experiencing oppression and prejudice in social, political, and educational structures of society.

Dominant Cultures, Oppression, and Other Societal Issues Affecting the Identity Development of Diverse Populations

"This work deals with a very obvious truth: just as the oppressor, in order to oppress, needs a theory of oppressive action, so the oppressed, in order to become free, also need a theory of action. The theory of oppression is learned, transmitted, and replicated."

(Freire, 1987, p. 185)

FOR MEMBERS OF RACIAL AND ETHNIC GROUPS, it is not the concept of adapting to the context that causes problems but the experience of oppression that leads "to marginalization, making it difficult for minorities to have a positive sense of their cultural identity, which is linked to self-esteem and other psychological variables" (Birman, 1994, p. 274). For this reason, the question of identity for diverse populations must begin with the reality of living in a dominant culture that has a history of oppression in the United States.

This chapter discusses concepts that frame the understanding needed to participate in the dialogue this monograph promotes. The first concept is the phenomenon of oppression and theories that have emerged to help us understand the process as well as the consequences of oppression. The second concept is how the privilege of being the dominant culture has influenced the identity development of whites in the United States. Together these two concepts lay the necessary groundwork.

The question of identity for diverse populations must begin with the reality of living in a dominant culture that has a history of oppression in the United States.

Cultural and Societal Issues That Impact Identity Development

Before faculty and administrators can begin to truly address issues related to identity development of diverse populations and design practices to empower these groups, a connection must be created between how behavior is shaped by outside influences and the oppression. To understand the racial and ethnic identity development of those who are considered nonmajority, it is important to understand how societal and cultural issues are intertwined with the feelings, thoughts, and fears of racial, ethnic, or other social subordinate groups. "These culturally subordinated and economically marginalized ethnic communities have struggled to forge their own positive American identity against presumptions of their racial inferiority" (Adams, 2001, p. 212). It is this struggle against racism and sexism that is captured in the theories of oppression.

Systematic racism and sexism is a central part of the foundation of our national identity, and its eradication requires the uprooting and changing of the existing hierarchy of power (Spring, 1994; Takaki, 1993). For change to occur in the majority culture, it must be acknowledged that one group historically has possessed power and used it to create negative racial stereotypes of the new groups. This notion of historical racial superiority justifies their oppression of others to maintain their advantaged status (Helms, 1994). For the cycle of oppression to change, whites (the majority culture) would have to lose some privilege and power. The recognition that some groups have privilege and power while others (minorities) do not is critical in understanding the development of individuals from racial, ethnic, and other social minority groups. Though many in higher education would like to see our society as accepting diverse populations, the historical media images of nonmajority people create a phenomenon that must be investigated to appropriately understand. A difficult yet important aspect of being nonmajority is the potential for experiencing oppression.

The theoretical framework provided in theories of oppression is needed for several reasons. According to Bell (1997), theory allows us to reason and think clearly about our intentions and how we implement our actions in various settings (classroom, residence hall, meetings, for example). It allows us time to think and mobilize our energy, then move in a direction of certainty. Theory can also mobilize social energy; a group of people can work toward a common goal grounded in theory; without such a base, personal dominance may become the focal point. Second, old approaches to interacting with individuals can be queried and challenged and new paradigms created when we infuse oppression theory with our actions. In other words, theory protects us against our own unconsciousness. "Ideally we keep coming back to and refining our theory as we read and reflect upon the emerging literature on oppression, and as we continually learn through practice the myriad ways oppression can seduce our minds and hearts or inspire us to further learning and activism" (Bell 1997, p. 4). Last, oppression theory reminds us that people are historical subjects and therefore history impacts the way we think, act, and behave toward others. It is important that we "learn from the past as we try to meet current conditions in more effective and imaginative ways" (Bell, 1997, p. 4).

Theory protects us against our own unconsciousness.

Theory of Oppression

According to Paulo Freire (1987), oppression is overwhelming control; "an act is oppressive only when it prevents [people] from being more fully human" (p. 42). Further, Freire states that the oppressors see only themselves as "human beings" and other people as "things." "For the oppressors, there exists only one right: their rights to live in peace, over against the right, not always even recognized, but simply conceded, of the oppressed to survival. And they make this concession only because the existence of the oppressed is necessary to their own existence" (p. 43). Those who are oppressed live in a culture of silence or have no voice when determining their destiny; thus, they are politically and economically powerless (Spring, 1999). The oppressed develop a mental construct called "the wheels in the head" syndrome (Spring, 1999). Oppressed people develop this thought process when their internalized ideas are not their own but rather are thoughts prescribed by others to subjugate them. Oppressed people are not independent thinkers controlling their own destiny; their future is determined by the oppressor.

The method most commonly used to dictate prescribed thoughts and minimizing creative power to oppressed groups is called *education as banking* (Freire, 1987). Teachers dictate information to the learners that is from an oppressive historical ideology. The learners become passive by not talking, sharing, or having dialogues with others; conversely, they receive, memorize, and repeat what has been dictated, thus creating a system where those in power deposit information and the oppressed are passive receivers of the information. When education as banking exists, the oppressed groups become the objects of history rather than the subjects. "A subject of history is a conscious maker of history" (Spring, 1999, p. 148). "As objects of history, their actions are determined by history, but they do not make history" (p. 148). This is a form of deculturalization or the educational process of destroying a people's culture and replacing it with a new culture (Spring, 2001).

When people accept oppression in their lives, they become dehumanized and lack any will, consciousness, or motivation to make societal or systematic changes (Freire, 1987). Without the critical consciousness to become self-determining rather than self-deprecating, the oppressed will continue to allow the oppressor to make choices for them that will limit their freedom. Even when a collaborative breakthrough occurs between the oppressors and the oppressed, praxis—the point when dialogue, reflection, and action transpire between the oppressors and the oppressed to transform the world—still needs to occur (Freire, 1987).

Overall, oppression consists of six significant themes (Bell, 1997, pp. 4–5):

1. Pervasiveness: Oppression is the pervasive nature of social inequality woven throughout social institutions as well as embedded within individual consciousness.
2. Restricting: Oppression represents structural and material constraints that significantly shape a person's life chances and sense of possibility.
3. Hierarchical: Oppression signifies a hierarchical relationship in which dominant or privileged groups benefit, often in unconscious ways, from the disempowerment of subordinated or targeted groups.

4. Complex, Multiple, Cross-Cutting Relationships: Power and privilege are relative, as individuals hold multiple and cross-cutting social group memberships.
5. Internalized: Oppressive beliefs are internalized by victims as well as benefactors.
6. "Isms": Shared and Distinctive Characteristics: Oppression is manifested through racism, sexism, classism, anti-Semitism, ableism, and heterosexism and the dimensions of experience that connect "isms" in an overarching system of domination.

Later models of oppression took these themes and applied them to specific societal contexts. The next model discusses these themes in the context of a society where one social group denigrates another social group to promote larger gains for themselves.

The Social Oppression Matrix

According to Hardiman and Jackson (1997), "oppression is not simply an ideology or set of beliefs that assert one group's superiority over another, nor is it random violence, harassment, or discrimination toward members of target groups" (p. 17). These researchers designed a social oppression model that is pervasive when one social group, consciously or subconsciously, denigrates another social group for its own gain (Hardiman and Jackson, 1997). Four key elements take place when social oppression occurs:

1. The agent group has the power to define and name reality and determine what is "normal" and "real" or "correct."
2. Harassment, discrimination, exploitation, marginalization, and other forms of differential and unequal treatment are institutionalized and systematic. These acts often do not require the conscious thought or effort of individual members of the agent group but are rather part of business as usual that becomes embedded in social structures over time.
3. Psychological colonization of the target group occurs through socializing the oppressed to internalize their oppressed condition and collude with the oppressor's ideology and social system.

4. The target group's culture, language, and history are misrepresented, discounted, or eradicated, and the dominant group's culture is imposed.

Social oppression exists when one group is the beneficiary of privileges because of their social group membership (Hardiman and Jackson, 1997). These privileges are supported by institutions and structures of a society as well as by individuals who assist in the operation, support, maintenance, and perpetuation of these benefits. Hardiman and Jackson's Social Oppression Matrix (1997) comprises individual, institutional, and cultural/societal levels. These levels work in a dynamic fashion along three dimensions (context, psychosocial processes, and application) to sustain and strengthen each other (Hardiman and Jackson, 1997).

The context axis intersects with the individual, institutional, and cultural/societal levels. The boundaries are fluid, allowing for interaction and thus making all three levels equally supportive. The individual level emphasizes the beliefs, views, values, and practices of one person rather than an entire social or institutional system. The impact of social oppression on an individual and the institution is reciprocal. Individuals are impacted by the institution when they abide by, maintain, and sustain oppressive rules, regulations, and structures. Conversely, individuals have a direct interaction with the institution when the dominant societal values, codes, and mores are internalized and valued.

Institutions such as corporations, schools, colleges, and universities, religion, local, state, and federal government and the family construct are impacted by two levels. "The application of institutional policies and procedures in an oppressive society run by individuals or groups who advocate or collude with social oppression produces oppressive consequences" (Hardiman and Jackson, 1997, p. 19)—for example, policies barring people of color from country clubs or the exclusion of women from primary roles of power in religious organizations.

The psychosocial processes may be conscious or unconscious when individuals decide to support, collude, or actively participate in a system of social oppression (Hardiman and Jackson, 1997). People act as conscious participants in social oppression when they engage in activities that support and maintain a system that denigrates others, for example, providing funds for a white supremacist group or voting against human rights legislation. Unconsciously, individuals may be acting in a naive or unsuspecting manner when they support culturally demeaning social norms, such as people of color changing their nose or lips through plastic surgery to mirror white features.

The application dimension recognizes that social oppression is evident at the behavioral and attitudinal levels of individual and system interface (Hardiman and Jackson, 1997). "The attitudinal level describes the individual and systemic values, beliefs, philosophies, and stereotypes that feed the other dimensions" (p. 19), for example, stereotypes of Irish as drunks, Italians as belonging to the Mafia, white people as having no rhythm, and white men as being unable to jump. An individual who believes the stereotypes promotes processes that maintain rather than diminish these stereotypes. When zoning laws are designed to keep poor children in dilapidated schools or people of color are systematically overlooked for promotion and relegated to low-paying positions, individuals are taking actions that sustain and preserve social oppression.

Social Identity Development Theory

Social identity development theory (Hardiman and Jackson, 1997) details the characteristics common to the identity development for oppressed and dominant groups. It is suggested that the theory not be used to label people, because they may be in one or more stages simultaneously, coping with different emotional and cognitive struggles with oppression. The theory is helpful in understanding the perspectives of students and developing training or teaching modules.

Naive/no social consciousness is the first stage of the theory in which individuals from oppressed and dominant groups "are unaware of the complex codes of appropriate behavior for members of their social group" (Hardiman and Jackson, 1997, p. 23). They may experiment and push the boundaries or norms, but the social structure provides information and cues about what it is like to be part of a particularly social category. They begin to accept the roles prescribed by teachers, parents, clergy, or the media and note differences between and among individuals.

In the second stage, *acceptance,* these roles are internalized, and the oppressed and dominant groups conform to the characteristics society has deemed appropriate for them, whether conscious or unconscious. Members of the dominant group of the passive acceptance stage "have learned to some degree internalized codes of appropriate behavior, [and] conscious effort is no longer required to remind them of what to do and how to think" (Hardiman and Jackson, 1997, p. 24). If members of the dominant group are in the active acceptance stage, they receive messages in a very overt and direct method that people from oppressed groups are inferior, deviant, and weak. Privileges are evident for dominant members of the active acceptance stage, although they are oblivious to these societal perks. Oppressed people in the acceptance stage have learned to internalize and accept messages about the inferiority of their culture and themselves. Passive acceptance individuals are oblivious to how they emulate the oppressor and reflect their views. Oppressed persons in the active acceptance stage overtly or consciously connect with the views, beliefs, and ideology of the dominant group.

Increased awareness occurs in the *resistance* stage of awareness. In this third stage, members of the dominant group have experienced a challenging life event that provides some impetus for creating a new worldview and rejecting their old frame of reference. Those persons who are oppressed begin to acknowledge and question the collective experiences of oppression; their damaging effects lead these individuals to the resistance stage.

Stage four, *redefinition,* requires that a new identity be created "that is independent of an oppressive system based on hierarchical superiority and inferiority" (Hardiman and Jackson, 1997, p. 27). Dominant group members start to reframe and create new definitions for their social group identity that is autonomous from social oppression and to project prejudicial views onto oppressed groups. Members of the oppressed group find themselves independently defining who they are and developing a new personal identity in the redefinition stage. This stage is significant for the oppressed, because "it is at this juncture that they shift their attention away from a concern for their interactions with agents towards a concern for primary contact with members of their own social group who are at the same stage of consciousness" (p. 27).

The final stage, *internalization,* is geared toward infusing the identity developed in the redefinition stage into every phase of one's life. The dominant groups work toward creating a more inclusive and egalitarian society. The oppressed groups are engrossed in embracing and accommodating their new level of critical consciousness and group dignity.

How Oppression Impacts Privileged Groups

Oppression has a tremendous impact on the identity development of dominant or privileged groups. McIntosh (1998) metaphorically describes white privilege as "an invisible package of unearned assets that I could count on cashing in each day but about which I was meant to remain oblivious. White privilege is like an invisible knapsack of special provisions, maps, passports, codebooks, visas, clothes, tools, and blank checks" (p. 207). Based on McIntosh's insights, it is important that the impact of oppression and privilege on dominant groups be explored from multiple aspects, specifically psychological, social, moral and spiritual, intellectual, material, and physical (Goodman, 2001).

When social systems of oppression constrain people and keep them from becoming fully human, the psychological cost is a loss of mental health and authentic sense of self (Goodman, 2001). The psychological costs manifest themselves in the following ways:

- Socialization into roles and patterns of behaviors: People in dominant groups are socialized to conform to certain rigid standards of behavior.
- Denial of emotions and empathy: Personal growth is further limited when people attempt to deal with the contradiction between what they are often taught (equality, love, and kindness) and what they are expected to do (treat people inequitably).
- Limited self-knowledge and distorted view of self: People from privileged groups are routinely denied information and opportunities to understand their role in an unjust social system as well as honest feedback from people in oppressed groups.

- Discrepancy between external perceptions and internal realities: Individuals do not feel like the powerful, privileged people they are presumed to be. Even though there may be material success, there can be emotional and spiritual emptiness.
- Fear and pain: There are fears of losing entitlement and power, the fear of losing respect within the dominant culture if they collude with the oppressed. There is pain when privileged groups that support justice are witness to a hostile or violent incident towards the oppressed group.
- Diminished mental health: People from dominant groups tend to develop unhealthy psychological mechanisms (such as denial, false justification, projection, disassociation, and transference of blame) to deal with their fears of minorities or people from oppressed groups. [Goodman, 2001, pp. 106–107]

In the category of social costs, relationships are lost and diminished when the dominant group lacks trust between groups, thus creating a climate that does not support boundary breaking and forging friendships (Goodman, 2001). Societal costs occur through isolation from people who are different, barriers to deeper and more authentic relationships, and disconnection, distance, and ostracism within one's group.

Societal costs occur through isolation from people who are different, barriers to deeper and more authentic relationships, and disconnection, distance, and ostracism within one's group.

The nonrecognition of privilege entails critical moral and spiritual costs (Goodman, 2001), specifically the loss of integrity and a spiritual center. Guilt and shame surface when a person has more material goods than another, moral ambivalence when they begin to face family and societal disapproval for questioning the status quo, and spiritual emptiness or pain when the actions of the oppressor are not part of the spiritual philosophies one lives by.

The intellectual cost of oppression to people from dominant groups is the loss of developing a full range of knowledge (Goodman, 2001). They remain miseducated, uninformed, and ignorant of their own culture and history and that of the oppressed groups. Finally, the material and physical costs of oppression are loss of safety, resources, and quality of life (Goodman, 2001). When people are oppressed, they may inflict harm and violence on the oppressor in the form of social unrest or the creation of enough tension that people must fear for their safety. When oppressed people become desperate for food, shelter, and other necessities of life, they may turn to stealing or causing physical harm to those in power or those who seem to have material wealth, leading to higher costs for people who wish to live in safe and comfortable neighborhoods and a waste of resources, because tax dollars are spent incarcerating angry people who were denied the opportunity to live a life similar to those who are privileged. Most important, the privileged people experience negative health implications because they may "experience high degrees of stress and stress related illnesses as they feel increasingly fearful and disconnected from other human beings. Pressures to achieve and maintain status in a hierarchical and competitive social and economic system further undermine health" (Goodman, 2001, p. 119).

This understanding of a society that oppresses prompts a closer look at the identity white people develop. White identity development models are a guide to understanding the process necessary to engage in cross-cultural communication, dialogue, and action to transform society.

White Identity Theories

White identity development and the issues of privilege, oppression, and white racism have been discussed frequently with a renewed amount of energy in the past ten years (Feagin, 2000; Goodman, 2001; Hobgood, 2000; McIntosh, 1998; Wellman, 1993). Researchers and theorists are restructuring older theories (Hardiman, 2001; Helms and Cook, 1999) or presenting challenging new concepts (Ortiz and Rhoads, 2000). White faculty, administrators, and students are connected to a racial group that has, according to McIntosh (1998) and Hobgood (2000), amassed a great many unearned privileges. One privilege is being socialized that whites have no race and that "the word 'race' [refers] to other people. I was just 'normal'" (McIntosh, 1998, p. 214). Helms and Piper (1994, p. 126) provide the following definition of a white person: "those Americans who self-identify or are commonly identified as belonging exclusively to the White racial group regardless of the continental source (e.g., Europe, Asia) of that racial ancestry."

White racial identity development theories acknowledge that the theories are based on how whites perceive other racial ethnic groups and not their own (Hardiman, 2001; Helms and Cook, 1999; Ortiz and Rhoads, 2000). The understanding of attitudes and behaviors white people internalize and believe is not new, but the study of their racial identity development from an interpersonal and cognitive perspective is the focus of recent research. White identity is constructed within a complex set of interconnecting social locations (for example, race, class, and gender), and it is shaped by social, economic, and historical processes. Earlier models of white identity development (Hardiman, 2001) "required an understanding of the way oppression impacts individuals, rather than from a 'cultural difference' analysis in which the focus is directed at White identification with White culture" (p. 111).

The white identity model conceptualized by Hardiman in the early 1980s and then revised in the 1990s has five stages (Hardiman, 2001):

1. No social consciousness of race or naïveté about race: Whites do not understand the construct of race or the social understanding of racial differences. The naïveté about race ends around childhood.
2. Acceptance: Living in this society, covert and overt messages of white privilege are prevalent and whites begin to accept or internalize a sense of superiority over others.
3. Resistance: There is a realization at this stage that the dominance of one group over another is wrong, and there is an effort to question and resist the racist messages being constantly presented.
4. Redefinition: The white attempts to redefine and take responsibility for her/his whiteness and takes a personal interest in fighting racism.
5. Internalization: Consciousness has been elevated at this level and a new white identity created that is aware of racial and social injustices.

Hardiman notes that the stages are a prescription of what whites should do rather than a description of personal shared experiences by all white people.

Another model of white racial identity development was created by Janet Helms (1992) that has six statuses, each building in purpose and dimension. The first status is *contact,* which is where "the racial identity evolutionary process for Whites begins" (Helms and Cook, 1999, p. 91). Behaviors of this stage are an obliviousness to being in a racial group and issues related to privilege. In the second status, *disintegration,* whites encounter a moral dilemma that thrusts them into seeing discrimination in society. The dilemma is choosing group loyalty and obliviousness or being socially conscious of the inequities. The third status, *reintegration,* is "a system for mitigating the anxiety that occurs when one's Disintegration status is dominant" (Helms and Cook, 1999, p. 92). A decision is made to maintain the white racial status quo and avoid any personal responsibility for ending racism at this level. *Pseudo-independence,* the fourth status, has the white person identifying good nonracist persons of the race and bad racist persons, thus separating from the racists. *Immersion,* the fifth status, involves the search for a positive definition of whiteness. The sixth status, *emersion,* is a rejuvenation process that involves removing oneself from the whites who are insensitive to racial issues and delving into a community that attempts to be reeducated about diversity, race, and multiculturalism. The final status, *autonomy,* "permits complex humanistic reactions to internal and environmental racial information based on a realistic, nonracist, self-affirming conception of one's racial collective identity" (Helms and Cook, 1999, p. 93).

The dilemma is choosing group loyalty and obliviousness or being socially conscious of the inequities.

Terry (1977), Carney and Kahn (1984), and Rowe, Bennett, and Atkinson (1994) have written other white racial identity development models, but Hardiman's model (2001) and Helms's model (1994) have been cited frequently or empirically tested the most. Ortiz and Rhoads (2000) designed a framework for multicultural education that explores and deconstructs whiteness. "If educators want to advance students' understanding of White privilege, and relatedly, racial inequality, they need to help students explore and deconstruct White racial identity, both among Whites and non Whites. This is a pivotal step in promoting a multicultural perspective" (Ortiz and Rhoads, 2000, p. 82). The framework for multicultural education (Ortiz and Rhoads, 2000) is a five-step, nonlinear process to be used as an educational intervention or curriculum development guide: (1) understanding culture—the person attempts to gain a deeper understanding of culture and how it shapes all of our lives, (2) learning about other cultures—the need to learn and explore diverse cultures at a deeper level, (3) recognizing and deconstructing white culture—the attempt to understand the universal nature of white privilege and to challenge what has been considered the norm, (4) recognizing the legitimacy of other cultures—the recognition that all cultures make a significant contribution to society, and (5) developing a multicultural outlook—reconstruction of the systems operating in the United States if society is to embrace all cultures.

The framework for multicultural education helps white students gain an understanding of their own culture as well as others by placing them in challenging situations and thought processes but with supportive individuals guiding them through their journey of intercultural enlightenment. The most important step in each model is for whites to become more introspective and understand that a race is a nice thing to have, according to Helms (1992). Hardiman (2001) stresses that the current research on white identity development has not explored the intersections of racism, privilege, and internalized dominance or the search for cultural meaning and identification. "Instead it focuses almost exclusively on the dominance or racism aspect of White identity, and gives scant attention to the way Whites identify in a cultural sense with their race" (Hardiman, 2001, p. 124). It is important for Whites to become comfortable with their white racial identity, because the demographic changes in society have occurred and our diverse cultures are becoming more predominant on college campuses. McIntosh discusses, for example, how disconcerting and dissonance provoking it must be for heterosexual white males to be told that having "maleness" is a problem and then "whiteness" and then "straightness" (1998, p. 215). "I think that many people who are trying to be reflective are feeling a kind of epistemological nausea from being whirled around so suddenly, as it seems to them. And I myself find that a retreat from the subject of being consciously white is tempting. I see it as curling up and falling asleep, and sleep has its place. But nightmares will come. And I would rather be awake, and not a sleepwalker. I now feel that being a white sleepwalker through the world of white control perpetuates a zombielike incapacitation of the heart and mind" (McIntosh, 1998, p. 215).

The work involved in gaining an appreciation for one's white racial identity is the first critical step in moving society into universal racial harmony and understanding. Unless white racial identity development is presented at all educational levels, teaching college students about affirmative action, racial equality, gender privilege, and other issues of oppression may fall upon deaf ears.

Conclusion

This chapter provides an overview of Freire's pedagogy of the oppressed, a social oppression matrix, the social identity development theory, and the impact of privilege on dominant groups. The context presented focuses on why identity development is difficult and why those who are oppressed often express different views about their experiences. This context is a critical foundation to understanding identity development among diverse populations. In addition, the white identity development models help with an understanding of the process necessary to engage in cross-cultural communication and thus promote constructive dialogue to transform society. This understanding of privilege is a critical element of the dialogue to promote a positive campus environment.

Through this overview, students, teachers, and administrators may be able to find creative and collaborative methods for reducing oppressive actions in the classroom and on campus. Additionally, personal reflection on the issue of social oppression may bring about a change in identity for some readers, who have not considered their own race through this lens.

Theoretical Frameworks of Diverse Identity Development Theories: A View Through a Different Lens

I N AN EFFORT TO ADDRESS the special developmental needs diverse students face during the college years, new theories have emerged that help us understand the experiences of these students. To cover the large variety of theories that have emerged in the recent literature, this chapter begins with the broad theories that apply to multiple ethnic and racial groups and then focuses on theories specific to a certain ethnic or racial group. Both must be considered to gain the knowledge necessary to deal with diverse populations.

Multigroup Ethnic and Racial Identity Models

We begin from the premise put forth by Sue and Sue (1999) that not all ethnic groups or cultures are the same. "Most would agree that Asian Americans, African Americans, Latino/Hispanic Americans, and American Indians each have a distinct cultural heritage that makes then different from each other" (p. 123). The word *multigroup* is meant to distinguish those theories that have been developed to look at the broad concept of being from a minority group versus those theories that have been created to describe a specific group of people. The broad ethnic or cultural identity models can provide a basis for explaining individual differences.

The study of ethnic identity development has furthered our understanding of how individuals make meaning out of the general question, "who am I?" Phinney (1996) explains this notion by stating that "in contrast to approaches that aim at objective descriptions of particular ethnic groups, the study of ethnic identity involves an emphasis on how group members themselves understand and interpret their own ethnicity" (p. 143). It is an important developmental process that we often see manifested in individual students throughout the college experience.

Atkinson, Morten, and Sue

Atkinson, Morten, and Sue (1979, 1989) outlined the minority identity development (MID) model that the authors believe spans the identity development issues of many groups of individuals. Sue and Sue (1990) refined and expanded the MID, renaming it the racial/cultural identity development (R/CID) model. This model is best viewed as a "conceptual framework" (Sue and Sue, 1999, p. 128) for interpreting the behaviors and attitudes of persons from various cultural and ethnic groups.

The R/CID model (see Figure 1) is a five-stage progression of development from *conformity* (or that period of time when one values the majority culture members and values above his or her own) to *integrative awareness* (when the individual has developed a strong sense of self as an individual and group

FIGURE 1
The Behavioral Patterns of Multicultural Competence Model

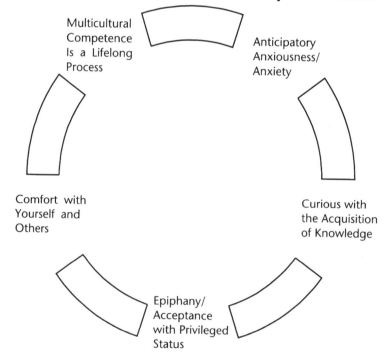

Multicultural Competence Is a Lifelong Process

Anticipatory Anxiousness/ Anxiety

Comfort with Yourself and Others

Curious with the Acquisition of Knowledge

Epiphany/ Acceptance with Privileged Status

member). Each stage in the model involves four attitude or belief processes: (1) attitude about self, (2) attitude toward other members of the same minority group, (3) attitude toward others of different minority groups, and (4) attitude toward dominant group members.

During *conformity*, the majority culture (primarily white culture) represents the desired outcome. The ethnic or cultural group member seeks ways to fit in, takes on majority culture values, and holds everything in the majority culture as superior to his or her own. In fact, the opposite reaction can also occur: The person is ashamed of or embarrassed by characteristics of his or her own culture. Movement from this stage to the next, or *dissonance*, occurs when a conflict begins to be felt by the individual or through a more traumatic event that pushes him to reconsider previously held beliefs. In their description of this model, Robinson and Howard-Hamilton (2000) note that "for people of color, this is a fatiguing stage as tremendous energies are used to resolve conflicts toward the self, the same racial group, and the group in the majority" (p. 82).

The *resistance and immersion* stage is a complete reversal of the first stage that is caused when the individual moves completely toward acceptance of her or his culture, the minority point of view, and rejects the majority culture. Reactions here can also be strong and emotionally intense as racial pride swells. Some individuals even limit interactions with whites, preferring only to socialize with, purchase products and services from, and work with other members of their ethnic group. The person in this stage is very interested in acquiring more knowledge about his or her cultural heritage. There is now a strong sense that the majority culture is the oppressor and responsible for any inequities encountered by the minority culture.

> **Reactions here can also be strong and emotionally intense as racial pride swells.**

The fourth stage of the R/CID model is *introspection*. There is a movement away from group identification and anger toward majority culture to more personal reflection. According to Sue and Sue (1999), "The individual begins to discover that this level of intense feelings is psychologically draining and does not permit one to really devote more crucial energies to understanding themselves or to their own racial/cultural group" (p. 135). This does not mean that the feelings of frustration and ethnic pride attained in previous stages are diminished, only that feelings, values, and beliefs are weighted in relation to potential individual outcomes.

The fifth stage is *integrative awareness*. Here the individual has a well-defined sense of self and can incorporate aspects of his or her culture and U.S. culture into her or his individual identity. The attitudes toward self become self-appreciating while still appreciating the group affiliation. This individual can now show "selective trust and liking for members of the dominant group who seek to eliminate oppressive activities of the group" (Sue and Sue, 1999, p. 137).

Phinney

Phinney (1990, 1992) has proposed a model of ethnic identity development that is based on general identity models such as Erikson (1968) and Marcia (1980) and other ethnic identity development models such as Atkinson, Morten, and Sue (1979, 1989). According to Evans, Forney, and Guido-Dibrito (1998), "Ethnic identity develops from the shared culture, religion, geography, and language of individuals who are often connected by strong loyalty and kinship" (pp. 79–80). Phinney, who conducted her research with minority youth, found that the development of an ethnic identity was closely tied to the process of resolving conflict between (1) the level of prejudice and stereotyping perceived as prevalent from the majority culture and (2) dissonance of values between minority and majority culture. The resulting three-stage model of ethnic development closely resembles Marcia's four-part model of identity development.

The first stage of her model, *unexamined ethnic identity*, is a period of time when individuals need to explore beliefs and attitudes about their own ethnicity. If the result of this exploration is to accept what they have heard from others without question, then foreclosure occurs. If, however, they do not see their ethnicity as an important part of who they are as individuals in society, then the result is identity diffusion.

Ethnic identity search/moratorium is the second stage of Phinney's model. In this stage, individuals become more interested in their ethnic heritage. They consider the values displayed by significant others in their surroundings, read information that calls their values into question, and have sustentative conversations or periods of reflections about what it means to a member of their ethnic group. At times, this stage can evoke strong emotions in the individual, which can be characterized as the release of internalized anger toward the majority culture that is now viewed as the oppressor. The important part of this stage is making ethnicity more than an abstract concept: It is now a personal feeling that becomes congruent with behaviors.

Stage 3, *ethnic identity achievement,* results from the exploration of what it means to be a member of an ethnic group and make the commitment to group membership. A bicultural identity develops whereby individuals achieve a level of comfort with who they are in society.

A follow-up study supported the sequential nature of development and the fact that those at the higher stages remain stable (Phinney and Chavira, 1992). The importance of ethnicity was also considered in a later study by Phinney and Alipuria (1990), in which ethnic identity was rated as equally important as religion and more important than political orientation. For white students, occupation and sex roles were considered more important.

Phinney (1992) developed an instrument for use in measuring this construct. The multigroup ethnic identity measure (MEIM) assesses dimensions of ethnic identity development, information acquisition or exploration, and level of commitment. The instrument has very strong reliability and validity information for use with a variety of individuals. More research is needed, however. Ponterotto, Casas, Suzuki, and Alexander (2001) point out several additional studies that could strengthen the psychometric properties of the instrument, including social desirability of the responses and exploratory and confirmatory factor analysis.

Myers, Speight, Highlen, Cox, Reynolds, Adams, and Hanley

The process described in the optimal theory applied to identity development (OTAID, Myers and others, 1991, p. 58) is one in which the individual moves from a fragmented worldview to a more complete one; this change in turn connects the individual to the greater community.

Six developmental phases of the OTAID illustrate the development of identity:

> Phase 0: Absence of Consciousness Awareness—It is. Individuals lack awareness of being. . . .
>
> Phase 1: Individuation—The world is the way it is. Individuals lack awareness of any view of self other than the one to which they initially introduced. . . .

Phase 2: Dissonance—I'm beginning to wonder who I am. Individuals affectively explore those aspects of self that may be devalued by others. . . .

Phase 3: Immersion—I focus my energy on people like me. Individuals fully embrace others like themselves who are devalued. . . .

Phase 4: Internalization—I feel good about who I know I am. Individuals have effectively incorporated feelings of worth associated with the salient aspects of self, resulting in an increased sense of security. . . .

Phase 5: Integration—With my deeper understanding of myself I am changing my assumptions about the world. Individuals' sense of self has developed to a stronger place of inner security so that relationships and perceptions of others reflect this degree of inner peace. . . .

Phase 6: Transformation—It is I. The self is redefined toward a sense of personhood that includes the ancestors, those yet unborn, nature, and community. . . . [pp. 59–60]

Implications

These models suggest a fluid developmental process that students begin or continue to encounter and struggle with while in college. Students we work with or who are in our classrooms are at varying levels of their own identity development and ethnic identity development, presenting both opportunities and challenges for faculty and administrators to provide a safe environment where students feel encouraged to further explore these issues as individuals and with others. One of the challenges that faculty and administrators face is assessing students' level of readiness for this exploration and self-reflection. It is also important to illustrate for students their role is critical in creating a safe environment for growth. Assessing the level of

Assessing the level of readiness and providing a safe environmental setting provide the best balance of challenge and support to promote growth and learning among students.

readiness and providing a safe environmental setting provide the best balance of challenge and support to promote growth and learning among students.

Racial and Ethnic Identity Theories Pertaining to African American Students

The models presented in this section provide an overview of the racial and ethnic identity development process based on specific groups we may encounter on campus. These theories differ from the multigroup theories because they are based on a specific group. It is important to recognize that these theories are not all encompassing and that therefore not all students will "fit" in the stages of these theories. For example, Helms and Cook (1999) caution that "information about a person's racial identity does not reveal anything about her or his cultural socialization, except perhaps how much the person values her or his socioracial group's traditional culture" (p. 98). Students may display aspects of identity without having a complete understanding of the overriding political and social dimensions that are "central to their survival" (p. 98). The programming, course assignments, or individual conversations we have that challenge (and support) the student to go through this level of personal exploration will have positive payoffs to both the student and others in the institution.

Historically, African Americans were denied access to educational opportunities since the founding of the first colleges and universities in the 1600s (Anderson, 2002). It was not until after the Civil War that African Americans were allowed admittance into a few American higher education institutions. The 1954 *Brown* v. *Board of Education* decision enabled African Americans to broaden their search for an education at predominantly white institutions. The civil rights movement, in addition to the enactment of key federal legislation in the 1960s and 1970s, pushed the door open wider for people of color to be admitted at most U.S. institutions of higher education with financial assistance and programmatic support. To look at the racial identity development of black students, one must begin by recognizing the institutionalized racism that existed in the United States. College enrollment for African Americans increased by 38.6 percent from 1986 to 1996; students made up 7.2 percent of the enrollment in graduate schools in 1996 (Anderson, 2002). But one must ask what the quality of life was like for them on predominantly white campuses during the 1960s to 1980s when enrollments were high for black students.

Sedlacek (1999) conducted a germinal review of the research in 1987 on the quality of life for black students at predominantly white institutions. Several important findings from this literature base pointed to the fact that African Americans had continued difficulties with self-concept, racism, working with white faculty, and developing a community, to name just a few issues. Current research indicates that the collegiate environment for black students has not changed and that many variables still hinder their psychosocial and cognitive development.

Black students still find the environment at predominantly white colleges and universities to be racist (Feagin, Vera, and Imani, 1996). When compared with white students, most African American students view the campus to be more challenging and hostile (D'Augelli and Hershberger, 1993; Gloria and Pope-Davis, 1997; Perka, Matherly, Fishman, and Ridge, 1992), increasing their stress levels and leading to dissatisfaction and attrition (Feagin, Vera, and Imani, 1996; Lang and Ford, 1992; Pascarella and Terenzini, 1991). Even white students have very little contact with African American students, and most of their perceptions are based on preconceived stereotypes (Saddlemire, 1996).

Enough cannot be said about the relationship between a positive self-concept and the support of faculty, staff, and students in making the college environment comfortable for students who traditionally have been marginalized.

Gloria, Robinson Kurpius, Hamilton, and Willson (1999) found that "higher levels of social support, more comfort in the university environment, and positive self-beliefs would be associated with more positive academic persistence decisions of African American undergraduate students in predominantly White universities" (p. 263). Pope (1998) also noted that students' racial identity development and connection with the campus environment could influence their level of psychosocial development. African American students progress through stages of racial identity development, and the positive as well as negative energy expended in and out of the college classroom significantly influences their growth. Taylor and Howard-Hamilton (1995) found that African American males who become involved in extracurricular activities, particularly black Greek organizations, exhibit higher levels of self-esteem and racial identity development. Enough cannot be said about the relationship between a positive self-concept and the support of faculty, staff, and students in making the college environment comfortable for students who traditionally have been marginalized. Recognizing the steps of racial identity development could help the dominant culture understand the variations in psychosocial and cognitive growth of African American students.

Cross

Black American psychologists became intensely interested in attempting to observe, map, and label the identity transformation that accompanied a person's involvement in the black power movement from 1968 to 1975 (Cross, 1971, 1991, 1995). One such study became the psychology of *nigrescence,* a French word meaning the process of becoming black, "or rather, the gradual transcendence of Black individuals from a world view in which African Americans are devalued and Whites are reified to a world view characterized by an inner confidence in and appreciation of self and others as racial beings" (Thompson and Carter, 1997, p. 18). Nigrescence, in other words, is a series of experiences that resocializes a person's preexisting non-Afrocentric identity into an Afrocentric one (Cross, 1995). The development of research on nigrescence and the subsequent theory provides a detailed explanation of what occurs when a person goes through an identity transformation. Most important, black identity varies widely, and no uniform or unilateral form of thoughts and orientations exists among African Americans.

Cross (1971) originally developed a five-stage model of black identity development or nigrescence involving pre-encounter, encounter, immersion-emersion, internalization, and internalization-commitment. Each stage describes the psychological and behavioral characteristics of African Americans based on their interaction with societal oppression (Cross, 1971, 1991, 1995). Cross (1971, 1991, 1995) then revised his theory of nigrescence to take into account the cultural, social, psychological, and historical changes that had occurred over the twenty years since he first introduced the model. New language such as *race salience, personal identity,* and *reference group orientation* has been included in the behavioral and psychological description of individuals moving through the four, no longer five, stages.

Cross (1991, 1995) describes the first new term, *race salience,* as the level of importance, either low or high, of race to the individual. "Persons who hold low-salience views do not deny being physically Black, but consider this physical fact to play an insignificant role in their everyday life" (Cross, 1995, p. 98). *Personal identity* refers to "the general personality or overall self-concept common to the psychological makeup of all human beings and is considered a minor component in Nigrescence theory" (Vandiver, 2001, p. 167). Conversely, *reference group orientation* is a critical piece in understanding the theory, because it tells us about the social groups persons interact with to make meaning of who they are as social beings (Cross, 1991, 1995). Furthermore, nigrescence affects reference group orientation at four levels: "racial self-image, attitudes towards one's ascriptive group, choice of organizational membership, and ideology" (Cross, 1991, p. 161).

Stage 1: Pre-Encounter. Persons in this stage internalize low-salience attitudes toward being black. They do not deny being black but feel that their immutable characteristics play an insignificant role in how people interact with them (Cross, 1995). Another type of pre-encounter person is one who has the attitude that race is a social stigma or imposition. The individual has a superficial interest in black causes as a way of unifying with others who are trying to dismantle the social stigma connected with blackness. Another pre-encounter individual, antiblack, carries a high negative salience toward being black. The reason for this hatred is because of the western form of education that erased most positive images of black people from the textbooks and other materials. Additionally, the person has been socialized to prefer a Eurocentric cultural frame of reference. Therefore, the person adopts an assimilation-integration philosophy in which the pre-encounter black may oppose multicultural and diversity-sensitive education because it is nonessential information and not how the real world is structured. Finally, pre-encounter persons, according to Cross (1995, p. 103) "place priority on organizations and causes that have low race salience and or little nationalistic import, and

African Americans who are deeper into Nigrescence stress activities and organizations for which race and Black culture are highly salient." African Americans during the pre-encounter stage have a value structure and value orientation on affiliation with groups and beliefs toward certain causes, and they are no less communalistic than persons at the other stages.

Stage 2: Encounter. A series of micro assaults or crises causes the person at this stage to admit that the worldview that is valued now has flaws and the cumulative impact pushes the person toward nigrescence (Cross, 1995). This crisis entails a two-step process in which the person experiences the encounter and then personalizes it. The encounter need not be negative, but it must impact the person in a dynamic manner that will bring about strong emotions such as guilt, anger, shame, and anxiety.

Stage 3: Immersion-Emersion. This stage is the most critical and dynamic for persons attempting to clarify their black identity. During a problack and antiwhite identity when one enters immersion and emersion, merger and resolution of the dichotomous feelings occur (Cross, 1995). Feelings at the immersion phase are anger, guilt, and pride—anger and guilt for accepting and internalizing a white frame of reference that was psychologically and emotionally unhealthy and pride because they are learning about black heritage and it is affirming and empowering. Once self-actualization occurs, a transition into emersion occurs and with it a sense of altruism. At this phase, individuals understand that growth is a continuous process, and they are willing to experience the intense emotional phases that are tempered with wisdom and reflection. They are now able to move toward internalization of the new identity.

Stage 4: Internalization. Persons who move into the internalization stage have acquired inner peace, because they are no longer defensive about the social order of the world and their conception of blackness becomes more approachable, unrestrained, and refined (Cross, 1995). The cognitive dissonance experienced in the earlier stages has now dissipated, and a sense of dissonance resolution is present. Persons are comfortable with a variety of reference groups, and they can shift attention to other identity concerns such as gender, sexual orientation, religion, and multiculturalism. The internalized identity performs three critical functions: "(a) to defend and protect a person from psychological insults that stem from having to live in a racist society, (b) to provide a sense of belonging and social anchorage, and (c) to provide a foundation or point of departure for carrying out transactions with people, cultures, and human situations beyond the world of Blackness" (Cross, 1995, p. 113). Concomitantly, three internalization identities appear—black nationalist, biculturalist, and multiculturalist— appear, and regardless of which identity is internalized, there is a level of comfort with one's blackness (Vandiver, 2001). The black nationalist focuses on political and social issues impacting the African American community, the biculturalist has reference group orientations in two identities, usually blackness intersecting with another, and the multiculturalist identifies with blackness and at least two other cultural perspectives such as gender, sexual orientation, or a racial/ethnic group.

Stage 5: Internalization-Commitment. Cross (1991, 1995), Cross and Vandiver (2001), and Vandiver (2001) have stated that the fifth stage is actually a reiteration of activities, behaviors, and attributes of what the individual exhibits in the fourth stage. The research suggests collapsing the latter two stages together until further research has been designed to test the strength and validity of the fifth stage.

Overall, these stages are not linear, and movement does not occur in a step-wise progression. Some individuals may not ever move out of the first stage, and others may recycle continuously through the stages as life experiences dictate that behavior. African American students typically move through the stages of nigrescence throughout their lives, and their experiences in college can help or hinder this progression. The negative consequences of transition through the stages are regression, continuation/fixation at the third stage, and dropping out (Cross, 1995). Regression toward the pre-encounter stage occurs when persons become disillusioned and disappointed when growth is too challenging, negative, and nonreinforcing at the internalization stage. Continuation/fixation at the third stage is experienced by African Americans who are overwhelmed with hatred toward white people because their confrontations have been immensely painful. Some African Americans drop out of involvement with issues in their own communities and regress to pre-encounter, because fighting racism seems insurmountable and without solution.

Gay

Although Cross's nigrescence model is the most widely used for application to African American students, several other theories have explored black racial identity development. Gay (1984) developed a three-stage model based on socioracial identity and consciousness. During Stage 1, *pre-encounter,* individuals disconnect from their socioracial identity and embrace the characteristics exhibited by the dominant culture. Stage 2, *encounter,* finds these individuals faced with a socioracial identity crisis, and they are forced to begin a search for a group that supports the formation of a positive identity. In *postencounter,* Stage 3, the persons have developed a healthy socioracial identity and pride in the black culture.

Jackson

Approximately the same time Cross (1971) had conceptualized his nigrescence theory, Jackson (1976, 2001) developed five stages of black identity development or consciousness. Much like Cross, he has redeveloped his model to be consistent with the historical changes society has undergone, thus impacting how African Americans have transitioned over time (Jackson, 2001, pp. 15–16):

1. *Naive,* the absence of a social consciousness or identity;
2. *Acceptance,* suggesting the acceptance of the prevailing white/majority description and perceived worth of black people, black culture, or experience;
3. *Resistance,* the rejection of the prevailing majority culture's definition of valuing of black people and culture;
4. *Redefinition,* the renaming, reaffirming, and reclaiming of one's sense of blackness, black culture, and racial identity; and
5. *Internalization,* the integration of a redefined racial identity into all aspects of one's self-concept or identity.

Jackson felt the importance of restructuring the black identity development because of three social phenomenon that have occurred the past ten to twenty years: (1) issues of class resulting from a weakening economy that significantly impacts people of color, (2) the awareness of Afrocentricity that can be observed in the resurgence of celebrations such as Kwanzaa, and (3) the emergence of an understanding of ethnicity as well as race and "the effect they have on our self-concept and social interactions" (p. 26).

Banks (1981) created a five-stage model of black identity development in which the first step was *ethnic psychological captivity*. In this stage, the negative images and stereotypes of black people promoted by white society are internalized. During the *ethnic encapsulation stage*, African Americans find comfort in surrounding themselves with their own socioracial group. The next stage finds African Americans engaged in *ethnic identity clarification,* which is where self-love and acceptance emerge. Once individuals have a positive sense of self and love for one's own socioracial group, *biethnicity* occurs; thus, the individual can function comfortably in the world of the dominant culture and one's own. The last stage, *multiethnicity,* finds African Americans able to function in numerous cultural circles. Theories and models of black identity development typically stress the importance of a psychological rebirthing process that entails an immersion into one's own racial group.

Baldwin, Duncan, and Bell

Baldwin, Duncan, and Bell (1992) discussed the importance of heightened awareness for African Americans in the creation of their African self-consciousness construct. Specifically, "Black or African American (cultural) consciousness is central to normal and healthy Black personality functioning" (Baldwin, Duncan, and Bell, 1992, p. 284). The model has two core components: (1) the African self-extension orientation and (2) African self-consciousness. The African self-extension orientation is the spiritualistic core of the black identity system. "This spirituality, or *Africanity* as it is also called, is the key ingredient that allows for 'self-extension' to occur" (p. 284). The African self-consciousness component gives "conscious direction and purpose to the Africanity thrust that defines the core of the Black personality system" (p. 285). African consciousness also embraces four tenets (p. 285):

1. The recognition of oneself as "African" (biologically, psychologically, and culturally) and of what being African means as defined by African cosmology;

2. The recognition of African survival and proactive development of one's first priority value;

3. Respect for and active perpetuation of all things African, African life, and African institutions;

4. Having a standard of conduct toward all things "non-African" and toward things, people, and so on, that are "anti-African."

African American identity development has been promoted through the framework of Afrocentricity (Asante, 1987, 1991; Myers, 1988; Myers and Speight, 1994). The common Afrocentric worldview of Myers and Asante is quite similar to Baldwin, Duncan, and Bell's African self-consciousness construct—that there is a spiritual connection with all of life. Myers and Speight (1994) note that in understanding an Afrocentric worldview, "the self is multidimensional, encompassing the ancestors, those yet unborn, nature, and community" (pp. 103–104). Other connections involve interrelatedness, interdependence, and cooperation. In life, individuals seek an integrated and extended level of spirituality that is related to a higher level of development and identity.

Robinson and Howard-Hamilton

Robinson and Howard-Hamilton (1994) developed a recent model of identity development based on an Afrocentric resistance paradigm (Robinson and Ward, 1991) and the Nguzo Saba principles (Karenga, 1980), allowing African Americans a perspective that is more culturally congruent with their worldviews and value system. The model has seven principles, and unlike stage theories, these values promote psychological health and satisfying interpersonal relationships. Individuals can engage in one principle or all seven collectively: unity (*umoja*), self-determination (*kujichagulia*), collective work and responsibility (*ujima*), cooperative economics (*ujamaa*), purpose (*nia*), creativity (*kuumba*), and faith (*imani*). Finding healthy models of identity development for African Americans is critical; Collins (1990) believed that it is of tantamount importance for African American women.

African American feminist thought is a model of knowledge, consciousness, and empowerment for women of color, embracing the many dimensions of African American women. Collins (1990) asserts that diversity among

African American women has multiple contexts (race, class, gender, age, religion, and sexual orientation), from which these women's experiences can be revealed.

Implications

The significance of learning about and using different African American identity development theories is that, with so many variations of people in the black community, to assume that "one model fits all" would be a disservice to, for example, women of color who find that race, gender, and age are all salient identities and must be intersected. Varying models of racial identity development should be used because to fit a racial/ethnic group into one monolithic category does no more than what society has done for years—that is, generalize and stereotype a group of people based on the assumption that their behaviors, beliefs, values, and levels of consciousness are all the same. The use of racial identity theories is the first critical step for faculty, administrators, and students to develop the critical multicultural competency attribute of awareness. Through this lens, individuals can become cognizant of how people of color process and perceive the world. The role-taking perspective involved in applying theory to practice gives one insight into the pleasure and pain of being a person of color.

> **Varying models should be used because to fit a racial/ethnic group into one monolithic category does no more than what society has done for years—that is, generalize and stereotype a group of people based on the assumption that their behaviors, beliefs, values, and levels of consciousness are all the same.**

African American students experience social, systemic, and institutional oppression while attending predominantly white institutions. How the faculty, staff, and students react and interact with these students greatly impacts their racial identity development. Understanding the stages of nigrescence in combination with teaching practices and programming that are culturally responsive could raise the self-efficacy of black students and reduce racism and prejudice on campus (Howard-Hamilton, 2000).

Racial and Ethnic Identity Theories Pertaining to Native American Students

Non-Indians seldom recognize the diversity of American Indians. The federal government recognizes more then 481 tribes in the United States (LaCounte, 1987). Each tribe can have different language and customs. "Among Indians, identity development begins with the family, extended family, kinship, or clan affiliation" (Horse, 2001, p. 94). Thus, the developmental issues American Indians face in college are tied to the history of tribal sovereignty and the government-sanctioned oppression of native cultures in the United States. For this reason, it is important to understand how oppression of the native culture has influenced the identity development of American Indians.

Tribal sovereignty is critical to American Indians because of the history of government-sanctioned oppression of Indian culture. Many may feel that these issues are from the past, yet issues of sovereignty continue today and influence the available education for many American Indians. Though tribes have varying degrees of sovereignty, this governmental privilege provides tribal governments with some independence and the right to self-govern. Tribal sovereignty is based on the assertion that tribes had inherent sovereignty before there was a United States government and never delegated those rights to anyone else (Lomawaima, 2000). Tribal members take great pride in the notions of sovereignty; for many it is the "bedrock upon which any and every discussion of Indian reality today must be built" (p. 3). To understand American Indians, a person must respect their tribal affiliation and sovereignty—the first step in understanding the values that steer the identity of American Indians.

At the core of Indian values are communal concerns (including adherence to tradition), responsibility for family and friends, cooperation, and tribal identification (LaFromboise, Heyle, and Ozer, 1990). These values can conflict with the majority values of individualism, competitiveness, and amassing property. Those who work or teach American Indian students need to have a clear understanding of the central role these values play (LaFromboise and Rowe, 1983). The choices American Indian students make can be based on Indian values and may not necessarily be in line with the societal (majority white) values prevalent in the college environment. Three models can help faculty and administrators understand the identity development of American Indians. The first deals with categories of "Indianness," the second focuses on a healthy approach to acculturation into the majority culture, and the third focuses on factors that influence group consciousness.

LaFromboise, Trimble, and Mohatt

Building on the work of various researchers, LaFromboise, Trimble, and Mohatt (1990) classified Indians according to residential patterns, level of tribal affiliation, and extent of commitment to maintaining their tribal heritage. They identified five categories of Indianness:

> *Traditional.* These individual generally speak and think in their native language and know little English. They observe "old-time" traditions and values.
>
> *Transitional.* These individuals generally speak both English and the native language in the home. They question basic traditionalism and religion yet cannot fully accept dominant culture and values.
>
> *Marginal.* These people may be defensively Indian but are unable, because of their ethnicity, to live the cultural heritage of their tribal group or to identify with the dominant problems.
>
> *Assimilated.* Within this group are the people who, for the most part, have been accepted by the dominant society. They generally have embraced the dominant culture and values.
>
> *Bicultural.* Within this group are those who are, for the most part, accepted by the dominant society. Yet they also know and accept their tribal traditions and culture. They can thus move in either direction, from traditional society to the dominant society, with ease [p. 638].

Acknowledgment and awareness of the multiple loyalties inherent in American Indian students can assist non-Indians in understanding this group of students (LaFromboise, Trimble, and Mohatt, 1990). It is not clear what developmental process, if any, occurs within these categories, and it is therefore difficult to ascertain whether movement (or development) among the categories should be expected.

Choney, Berryhill-Paapke, and Robbins

The second model is Choney, Berryhill-Paapke, and Robbins's health model conceptualization of acculturation (1995). This model focuses on a health approach to acculturation rather than a deficit approach. The model represents four areas of human personality that are in harmony "with the domains of the medicine wheel (a uniquely Indian means of conceptualizing the human condition based on four essential elements)" (p. 85): behavioral, social/environmental, affective/spiritual, and cognitive. Within these areas are concentric circles, with the perimeter of each circle representing a different level of acculturation: traditional, transitional, bicultural, assimilated, and marginal. No value judgment is "placed on any level of acculturation, nor is any dimension of personality emphasized more than another" (p. 85). A person in each level would respond differently, illustrating the various ways of coping that result depending on an individual's environmental and societal circumstance. This model is not linear, and therefore it is feasible that an individual could maintain four different levels of acculturation when corresponding to the four personality domains.

Horse

Horse (2001) prefers to discuss Indian identity in terms of "factors that influence our individual and group consciousness as either tribal people or as American Indians" (p. 100). Five factors influence consciousness:

1. How well one is grounded in the native language and culture;
2. Whether one's genealogical heritage as an Indian is valid;
3. Whether one embraces a general philosophy or worldview that derives from distinctly Indian ways, that is, old traditions;
4. The degree to which one thinks of him or herself in a certain way, that is, one's own idea of self as an Indian person; and

5. Whether one is officially recognized as a member of a tribe by the government of that tribe [p. 100].

A person can meet four of the factors and not be recognized as a member of a tribe, because tribes are recognized as sovereign nations and have the power to act accordingly. This power includes determining who is or is not recognized as a member or citizen of a particular tribe (Horse, 2001).

Implications

This interaction between acculturation and personality domains is important to understand because American Indian college students may respond differently according to the personality domain and their own coping skills. For example, a student who is more acculturated in the cognitive domain yet more traditional in the social/environment domain may have few academic difficulties but many outside-class (social) stressors. Understanding the interactions among the developmental issues in the American Indian experience is critical to creating a positive environment for these students. These models can be useful in conceptualizing the variety of experiences that American Indian college students face and how reactions in the educational environment can be influenced by these choices. American Indians' experiences are becoming more varied, however, and may not be completely encompassed in these models.

Acculturation to the Majority Culture

The previous section on American Indians touched on the notion of acculturation to the majority culture. Before discussing the next two populations of students (Latino and Asian American), the construct of acculturation needs to be given further thought. The study of acculturation has existed since the late 1800s, when researchers considered the acculturation process of immigrants to the United States. Three types of models describe acculturation: (1) linear, (2) two-dimensional, and (3) multidimensional. These models express the nuances and greater understanding that researchers have about the process of adapting to broader social surroundings (Knight, Bernal, Garza, and Cota, 1993).

Linear models view the adaptation process on a continuum with polar extremes of positive ethnic identity and strong mainstream identification. These models are simplistic and assume that a stronger mainstream identification requires a weakened ethnic identification, but several studies have found it is not the case for ethnic students (Keefe and Padilla, 1987; Torres, 1999). *Two-dimensional models* consider the relationships with each culture simultaneously and independently. Some researchers consider two-dimensional models acculturation models, while others consider them bicultural models (Phinney, 1990). *Multidimensional models* recognize that the rate of acceptance and loss of some traits varies from trait to trait (Keefe and Padilla, 1987). This type of model looks at each cultural trait (food, language, music) and considers it independently on a continuum of absence or presence of the ethnic trait.

These models set the stage for the developmental choices students from noticeably different cultures can face. The process of choosing between the majority culture and their culture of origin places additional stress on how these students function in the college environment. The discussion of Latino and Asian student groups considers acculturation in their identity development process.

The process of choosing between the majority culture and their culture of origin places additional stress on how these students function in the college environment.

Racial and Ethnic Identity Theories Pertaining to Latino and Latina Students

The notion of a Latino identity is both controversial and complex. More than twenty countries of origin with distinct cultures claim the label Latino. The label Latino is used mainly in the United States to represent those who were born in or whose family originates in Central or Latin American and certain Caribbean countries. What these countries share is a colonial history that brought the Spanish language and other cultural traits (religion, some foods, and the mixing of indigenous, African, and

Spanish blood). It is the distinctive historical and societal context of Latinos in the United States that provides commonalities for Latino identity (Ferdman and Gallegos, 2001).

Two major factors influence the contextual history of Latinos in the United States: land boundaries and immigration. Because much of the West was once Mexico, some people of Mexican descent in the Southwest and West have been on U.S. soil for many generations. Yet like other minority groups, they have experienced institutional racism that oppressed their ability to express their culture and maintain their land rights. From the unwillingness to enforce the Treaty of Guadalupe Hidalgo to rules that punished school children if they spoke Spanish while in school, these institutionalized regulations have facilitated oppression of the Latino cultural identity until recently (Acuña, 1988).

The second major influence is immigration laws. Different countries have had different immigration status, making immigration easier or harder depending on which country one originates in. The desire to fight Communism in Cuba and some other countries created a unique immigration status for Cubans wanting to come to the United States, while economic and political issues in other countries made it more difficult for those individuals to migrate to the United States. Both these factors influence the societal and historical context of Latinos in the United States and have to be acknowledged before attempting to understand the identity development of Latinos in this country.

Theories dealing with Latinos in the United States tend to focus on one particular group (such as Mexicans or Puerto Ricans) or on the acculturation of Latinos. To provide an overview of available research, this section covers the theories that inform how Latino identity develops and models of biculturalism that provide information on college students.

Keefe and Padilla

Keefe and Padilla (1987) studied Chicano (Mexican American) ethnicity by looking at cultural awareness, ethnic loyalty, and ethnic social orientation. *Cultural awareness* focuses on an individual's awareness of Mexican people and culture. *Ethnic loyalty* represents perceptions and preferences that an individual develops about the Mexican culture, that is, an individual's attitudes and feelings about Mexican culture. *Ethnic social orientation* indicates the preference for interacting with others of Mexican descent and for ethnic foods.

Using a quantitative survey as their measurement tool, Keefe and Padilla (1987) found that cultural awareness decreases significantly between the first and second generations in U.S. participants and continues to decrease steadily through the fourth generation in the United States. Ethnic loyalty, however, has a very different effect, declining slightly between the first and second generations but remaining fairly constant through the fourth generation. This finding indicates that though individuals may not have knowledge of Mexican historical facts, they continue to maintain positive attitudes and feelings about their cultural origin. By the third or fourth generation, participants had higher ethnic loyalty scores than cultural awareness scores. A similar pattern was found with ethnic social orientation, indicating that even third and fourth generations in the United States continued to "associate primarily with members of their own ethnic group" (p. 52).

From this study, Keefe and Padilla (1987) created the Typology of Mexican American Ethnic Orientation. The five types range from Type I (unacculturated and identifying as Mexican) to Type V (extremely Anglicized and having little knowledge or identity with Mexican culture). The types in between are more difficult to distinguish, but most individuals are placed in Type III, a bicultural orientation that balances both cultures.

Torres

In a recent qualitative study of college students, Torres (forthcoming) interviewed students who self-identified as Hispanic or Latino to investigate the formation of Latino ethnic identity during the first two years of college. Torres found that students were very proud of their ethnic origin regardless of what conditions applied to their level of ethnic identity. Three conditions determine where Latino students are situated with regard to their ethnic identity when they begin college. The conditions that emerged during this longitudinal study shed light on how environment and personal choices influence the formation of Latino ethnic identity. Three conditions influenced ethnic identity in the first year: environment where they grew up, family and generational influences, and self-perception of status in society.

Environment where they grew up has a dimension that should be considered as a continuum. On one end of the continuum are the students who grew up in diverse environments; these students tend to have a strong sense of ethnicity and exhibit an openness to people from other cultures. On the other end are those students who grew up in a majority white environment; these students are more likely to associate with the majority culture (which does not mean they deny their culture of origin, only that they prefer the other culture).

Family influence and generational status focuses on two dimensions. First, students in their first year tended to use whatever label and description their parents use to describe their culture of origin. The second dimension focuses on the level of acculturation the student's parents had achieved. Because acculturation is heavily influenced by generation in the United States, these students tended to be categorized as (1) first generation in the United States or (2) second generation and beyond. For first generation in the United States students, their less acculturated parents created additional conflicts between the two cultures. These students were expected to balance the expectations of their parents with those of the college environment; many times these expectations conflicted with each other, while the second generation and beyond students had more acculturated parents and were better able to intermingle the two cultures, experiencing less stress over expectations in the college environment.

Self-perceived status in society focuses on the perceived privilege students felt growing up. This privilege should not necessarily be associated with social economic status, though in some cases a correlation may exist. Students who perceived they had some privilege tended to believe in the negative stereotypes about Latinos but did not see those stereotypes applying to themselves, while students who had no perceived privilege tended to be open to others and more likely to recognize racism in their environment.

Torres (forthcoming) found that two processes influenced change in students' identity. Change occurred when students experienced *conflict with culture* or when a *change in relationships within the environment* occurred. Each process has both positive and negative changes associated with them, depending on the issues students are dealing with. For example, conflict with culture that is based on not knowing the history of their country of origin can promote exploration in one student, while a cultural conflict with parents' views and expectations can promote withdrawal from the culture of origin for another student. The research found that students born outside the United States had to deal with both their own adaptation to the culture and their parents' adaptation to child rearing in a different culture. The incongruence between immigrant parents' expectations and societal norms provided additional stress and conflict for these students.

Similar interactions occur with changes in relationships. As students find congruence between their old learned beliefs and new beliefs, they establish relationships that better match this new identity. This change in relationships can be positive (if congruence is found) or negative (if conflict is not resolved).

Ferdman and Gallegos

This model of Latino identity development (Ferdman and Gallegos, 2001) focuses on the dimension of "defining one's orientation towards one's identity as Latino/a" (p. 49). The model is meant to serve as a framework to understand Latino identity development through its six orientations (Latino integrated, Latino identified, subgroup identified, Latino as other, undifferentiated/denial, and white identified), each one having a different lens, preferences, and views. This model uses the word *lens,* because it captures how individuals view their ethnicity and how they view the bigger picture of racial groups in the United States (Ferdman and Gallegos, 2001). The strength of this model is that it focuses on all Latino groups; its weakness is that it does not elaborate on development or how the lens are developed.

Bicultural Models

The concept of biculturalism is often used in the literature, yet no clear consensus exists on the meaning, process, or definition of biculturalism (Torres and Phelps, 1997). Abalos (1986) provides a simple definition, an overview of what occurs: Biculturalism is the synthesis of two cultures, out of which a third "reality" emerges that incorporates both cultures.

Using Latino populations, three theorists provide information useful for educators on the issues involved in choosing between two cultures. Szapocznik and Kurtines (1980) defined biculturalism as a two-dimensional acculturation model. Their findings on Cuban American students indicate that the more bicultural a student, the more likely the teacher would assign a high adjustment score. This finding prompted Szapocznik and Kurtines (1980) to suggest that maladjustment occurs when a bicultural individual is placed in a monocultural environment. This study provides insight but has limitations, because the sample included only Cubans.

The second bicultural model was created by Torres (1999; Torres, Winston, and Cooper, 2003; Torres and Phelps, 1997). This research found that the use of ethnic identity and acculturation measures could distinguish college students among four cultural orientation quadrants: bicultural orientation, Latino orientation, Anglo orientation, or marginal orientation. The study found, however, that no significant differences in levels of stress existed among the four orientations. This finding could indicate that there is no advantage in one orientation over another but that students cope with potential stress in different, yet equal ways. This study also suggests that Latino college students do maintain an ethnic identity even when they are more Anglo orientated in their behavior. The students' choice to associate more with the majority culture did not require them to diminish their identity with their culture of origin. The limitation of this model is that it is unclear about the process students experience in their choices. Because the model can only place students, more research is needed on the process used to choose between cultures.

The third study focused on creating an instrument that would identify the multidimensional construct of cultural identity among Latino and Latina adolescents (Feliz-Ortiz de la Garza, Newcomb, and Myers, 1995). Scales were developed to measure the multiple dimensions of cultural identity. The study produced an instrument with strong reliability, yet it was unable to discriminate among different cultural identity groups.

Implications

The diversity and historical/social context of Latinos in the United States greatly impacts how an individual Latino student may see himself or herself in the college environment. As a result, an educator needs to understand nuances among the cultures, historical issues within the cultures, and conditions that may impact individual Latino students.

Diversity in the Latino group requires sensitivity to country of origin and to generational status. The differences described by Torres (forthcoming) among students born in the United States and those born outside the country illustrate the different developmental issues students must contend with during their college experience. In addition, the migration pattern differs for each country, making their educational backgrounds very different (Lowell and Suro, 2002).

> **An educator needs to understand nuances among the cultures, historical issues within the cultures, and conditions that may impact individual Latino students.**

The best way to learn and understand these nuances is to ask students and to develop a trusting relationship with them so that they can discuss these difficult choices. With this information, an educator can respond to a Latino student in an informed and caring manner.

Racial and Ethnic Identity Theories Pertaining to Asian American Students

Ho (1987) and Huang (1994) note that Asian Americans are the most diverse ethnic group in the United States, making the study of ethnic identity development for this group challenging and complicated. A review of the literature also reveals some concepts that are not readily identifiable in research about other ethnic groups. Most notably, Yeh and Huang (1996), in their review of various Asian American ethnic identity development models, found that although "many theories suggest that ethnic identity development is predominantly an internal, intro-psychic process, our data [suggest] that Asian Americans are largely influenced by relationships and external forces" (p. 123). Several researchers have outlined ethnic identity development theories for specific Asian American groups. Kim's theory (1981) of Asian American identity development is often cited as a general theory applicable to all group members.

Kim

Kim (1981, 2001) found that the process of Asian American identity development in her sample of Japanese women involves five distinctly different stages that, like other psychosocial development theories, are sequential and progressive. The first stage, *ethnic awareness*, begins around the age of three or four years, before entering elementary school. According to Ponterotto and Pedersen's review of this theory (1993), children's attitudes toward being Japanese were either positive or neutral, depending on the extent of family involvement in ethnic activities. In the second stage, *white identification*, Asian American children begin to develop a sense that they are different from the whites with whom they begin to have increasing contact. This sense often results in being treated as inferior, which can lead to internalizing white societal values and becoming alienated from self and from other Asian Americans (Ponterotto and Pedersen, 1993). White identification can be "active," considering oneself very similar to white peers and not acknowledging cultural differences, or "passive," in which one does not consider oneself as white but does accept white standards, values, and beliefs as a reference point (Ponterotto and Pedersen, 1993).

During the third stage, *awakening to social political consciousness*, the individual sees him or herself as a minority in society and sheds previously held white-identified ideals. Self-concept becomes more positive and "centered on being a minority and they became politically conscious about being Asian American later" (Kim, 2001, p. 77). *Redirection to Asian American consciousness* begins when individuals start to embrace their Asian American identity and demonstrate a desire to immerse themselves in the Asian American heritage. During this period, individuals can feel anger or outrage at white society. In time, individuals work through the emotionally reactive phase and come to a reappraisal of themselves and other Asian Americans, feeling good about themselves, becoming proud to be Asian American. In the final stage, *incorporation*, individuals achieve a healthy, secure balance, feeling both comfortable with their own identity and appreciative of other racial groups, including the white majority. One develops a realistic appraisal of all people and does not feel a need to identify either with or against white people.

Ibrahim, Ohnishi, and Sandhu

Ibrahim, Ohnishi, and Sandhu (1997) adapted Atkinson, Morten, and Sue's MID model (1998) for use with South Asian Americans. They contend that the generic outline proposed by the MID and such other researchers as Kim (1981) and Uba (1994) is applicable to South Asian Americans, with the only exception for immigrant populations. Because immigrants from South Asia have experienced colonization by the British and also have a very strong ethnic identity, they can clearly see and accept the cultural differences between them and the host culture. Thus, for the immigrant generation, there is no *pre-encounter* or *conformity* stage in which they want to be part of the dominant culture, as "the acceptance of cultural differences is a reality of life for this group" (Ibrahim, Ohnishi, and Sandhu, 1997, p. 42). Because this group has also bought into the "American dream that hard work will overcome all differences" (p. 42), the *dissonance* stage for this generation comes when individuals realize that hard work is not enough, that cultural differences cannot be overcome, and that acceptance by mainstream Americans or other American-born ethnic minorities will not occur based on the perceived difference by mainstream America.

During *resistance and immersion,* the immigrant generation reverts to its Asian heritage and rejects all dominant culture and other ethnic minority assumptions and values, although Sue (1989) maintains that some Asian Americans at this stage may seek out temporary alliances with other minority groups that have been similarly oppressed. During *introspection,* South Asian Americans are sufficiently secure about their identity to begin to question previously held dogmatic beliefs. They also begin to seek their individuality as members of a minority group and to recognize some positive elements in the dominant culture. In the *synergistic* stage, Asian Americans have a strong sense of self-worth and individuality and are able to objectively accept or reject the cultural values of the dominant and the minority groups.

Maekawa Kodama, McEwen, Liang, and Lee

After reviewing the research literature for psychosocial themes and issues, Maekawa Kodama, McEwen, Liang, and Lee (2002) created a model of psychosocial development among Asian Americans. The model takes into account external influences from the dominant U.S. culture as well as those from traditional Asian cultures. The model is represented by placing *identity* at the center of an axis. The center of the axis represents the place a college student finds himself or herself, with two domains exerting influence. The two domains are on either side of the center and represent the dominant society and the traditional family/culture. "For some students, the distance between the two ends may be great, representing much incongruence between the dominant society and the values of their family. For others, the distance may be short, particularly if the student is relatively acculturated and feels little conflict between the domains of family and society" (Maekawa Kodama, McEwen, Liang, and Lee, 2002, p. 49).

This model attempts to depict how increased awareness of the pressures present within the axis can promote development of identity and thus promote change as well as growth in the individual student. The model is enhanced by five developmental tasks that are considered influences on identity: *emotions, competency, interdependence, relationships,* and *integrity.* Though this model encompasses some of the tasks found in Chickering's vectors (Chickering and Reisser, 1993), it also provides a critique of the vectors' application to Asian American college students (Maekawa Kodama, McEwen, Liang, and Lee, 2002).

Individual Differences

In addition to the effects of the college culture, identity development is a result of both individualized reaction to those cultural influences and characteristics unique to the various Asian American subpopulations. Yoshioka, Tashima, Chew, and Maruse (1981) identify at least twenty-nine distinct Asian American subgroups that differ from each other in language, religion, and values. Uba (1994) maintains that ethnic identity is more than a person's sense of belonging with other members of the ethnic group based on shared ethnic characteristics; it is a schema that (1) engenders general knowledge, beliefs, and expectations that a person has about his or her ethnic group; (2) functions as a cognitive, information-processing framework or filter within which a person perceives and interprets objects, situations, events, and other people; and (3) serves as a basis for a person's behavior.

Both these individual differences are represented in what Nicassio (1985) describes as the "salience" of ethnic identity (that is, the importance of ethnic identity within a conglomeration of identities). Having a salient ethnic identity does not necessarily indicate little acculturation. Many factors could affect the salience of ethnicity. One such factor could be attitude toward ethnicity. Feeling positive about ethnicity may relate to factors such as media portrayals of Asian Americans and parental attitudes toward ethnicity. A second factor that could affect ethnic identity is the concordance between the behaviors of other members of the ethnic group and a person's own behavior. Behaving in a way that is congruent with how one sees one's own ethnic group may increase the salience of ethic identity. For example, if part of the ethnic identity for Asian Americans is the belief that they earn good grades but some Asian Americans receive low grades, ethnic identity could lose some of its salience for the Asian Americans with low grades, and they may be less likely to invoke an ethnic identity.

A third factor that could influence variability in the salience of ethnic identity is the area in which a person resides or has attended school. For some people, the development of an Asian American ethnic identity depends in part on the social context, that is, whether there will be social support or understanding from the community if they invoke their Asian American ethnic identity. A non-supportive environment can provide a significant disincentive to the development of ethnic identity. A fourth factor that can account for variation in the salience of ethnic identity is the perception that Asian Americans have of other Asian American groups and of the dominant group. Uba (1994) describes three types of ethnic identity in addition to an identity as simply an American: (1) identification with Asian Americans as a group; (2) identification with one's specific Asian American group (for example,

A nonsupportive environment can provide a significant disincentive to the development of ethnic identity.

Chinese American or Filipino American); and (3) in the case of the foreign born, identification with people in a specific Asian country. The extent to which any of these three aspects of ethnic identity is demonstrated depends on the individual's perceptions of others and the degree to which he or she feels connected to those various "other" cultures.

A final factor that may affect ethnic identity is the extent of English language proficiency among immigrants in the Asian American subgroups. Maintaining one's native language, either excluding most English or bilingually, usually reinforces adherence to other cultural values, behaviors, and characteristics that inhibit acculturation and reinforce ethnic pride and continued identification with the native culture.

Implications

Given the diverse nature of the Asian American population on U.S. campuses, it is important to consider many factors in both group and individual interactions with students. It is critical that faculty and administrators keep in mind the importance of language, social context, relationships, and other external forces as influences on Asian identity development.

Multiracial Identity

The words *multiracial* and *biracial* are often used interchangeably (Kerwin and Ponterotto, 1995), yet they have some nuances. With multiracial identification, a person can identify with two (biracial) or more cultures with which they claim membership (Wijeyesinghe, 2001). The concept of identifying with more than one culture is not new; several theories consider multiracial identity development. This section offers a broad review of some theories and some new models that emerged recently. (For a good review of multiracial theories, see Wijeyesinghe, 2001.)

Poston and Kish

Poston (1990) considered biracial identity development in five stages: *personal identity, choice of group categorization, enmeshment/denial, appreciation,* and *integration.* The focus is on the individual's seeing value in having a multiple identity. Kish (cited in Kerwin and Ponterotto, 1995) focused on three stages:

awareness of differences and dissonance, struggle for acceptance, and *self-acceptance and assertion of an interracial identity.* Both authors provide insight into the process and choices an individual with more than one racial heritage must make, and both theories assume individuals will value and identify with the multiracial aspect of their identity.

A criticism of this approach is that these theories do not take into account the historical legacy of oppression in the United States, which has resulted in many multiracial people's being forced to select one race because of "socially imposed restrictions" (Wijeyesinghe, 2001, p. 136). Because of this criticism, Wijeyesinghe developed a model that focused on the factors that influence the choice of racial identity.

Wijeyesinghe

The factor model of multiracial identity (FMMI) identifies eight factors that impact the choice of racial identity (Wijeyesinghe, 2001): racial ancestry, cultural attachment, early experience and socialization, political awareness and orientation, spirituality, other social identities, social and historical context, and physical appearance (p. 137).

An individual's racial choice can be influenced by some or all of the factors. In addition, these factors are interrelated and can overlap. This model is recommended as a tool to organize the experiences of multiracial people and to assist in understanding the choices multiracial individuals make regarding racial identity. Wijeyesinghe (2001) warns that the FMMI can be misused if some factors are given more legitimacy than others. To keep this misuse from happening, those helping multiracial students should identify their own biases and beliefs about race and how those beliefs may influence their interaction with multiracial persons.

Dealing with multiracial individuals requires an understanding of the personal choices individuals have made about their own racial identification.

Implications

Dealing with multiracial individuals requires an understanding of the personal choices individuals have made about their own racial identification. More than other groups, multiracial students may struggle with being accepted by either group or not being sure which group they would like to identify with. It is also important to remember the pressure societal views of race can place on multiracial individuals. All these factors can come into play when dealing with a multiracial student.

Conclusion

This chapter has laid out many theories that deal with the experiences of racial and ethnic college students. Although more work has been done with some groups (African American) and less work with others (multiracial), the reality is that much more research is needed on all these groups. These theories draw from each other and at times build on each other. The fairly recent exposure of these theories is perhaps the main reason that much criticism has been published about them. As more research is conducted on diverse populations, more criticism and consensus may emerge on the identity development of diverse populations.

It is important to acknowledge the multiple layers that coexist within many students as they develop their identities. Now that the foundation for racial and ethnic identity has been set, the next chapter explores the interaction among the multiple layers of our identities.

Multiple Identities: Acknowledging the Interrelationship Among Roles

THE PREVIOUS CHAPTERS FOCUSED on identity development as though it occurred in a vacuum, with only that set of issues impacting development. It was necessary, however, to cover racial and ethnic identity theories first because they lay the foundation for understanding the interrelationship among the various roles students maintain. Racial and ethnic identity theories explain the central developmental task for many students, yet the reality is that multiple issues impact our identity. For example, Latinas may at times draw more on their Latino culture to express their identity and other times draw more on their identity as women. If the same woman experiences a situation at work where she feels she is being singled out or treated differently because of her gender, then her identity as a woman will be predominant in her thoughts about identity. These multiple identities help us understand the whole person.

Multiple identities help us understand the whole person.

Few individuals define themselves with just one identity; all of us simultaneously develop multiple identities throughout our life. We may be more aware of a particular identity and its effect, however, depending on what is occurring with us at a specific time. A frequently used metaphor for explaining an individual's identity is a radio dial. We all have many stations (identities) available. Sometimes, a station is very loud and needs our attention. At times, we need to turn up the volume to give our full attention to another station. At other times, we may listen more to one station than another, but all are operating, even if they are not what we are listening to at that time.

As previously noted, the traditional college-age years of eighteen to twenty-three are a time of focus on the development of identity. Answering the question "who am I?" is paramount and requires a substantial amount of reflection and action to try out new behaviors, consider alternative values sets, and become comfortable with the new roles students both take on and are given as college attendance nears completion. Often during this experimental period, students begin to understand the multiple layers (or stations) of identity they have to manage, develop, and make peace with to truly know who they are as individuals. Not as much research has been done in the area of multiple identities; therefore, we will tie together existing theories to illustrate the notion of multiple identities.

Some authors argue that to think of identity as singular (a particular station) does not encompass the complexity of this phenomenon. Rather than using the radio metaphor where we only hear one station at a time, perhaps we need to consider a multidimensional medium more like a symphony, where all identities (instruments) are playing at the same type to create a melody that varies in volume, intensity, and emphasis on various solos being played. If we believe this approach to be the case, then according to Raetz and Lease (2002), we should consider identity as:

- constructed (e.g., Deaux, 1993; Espiritu, 1994; Jones, 1997);
- grounded in social and cultural contexts (e.g., Chan, 1989; Cross, 1987; Deaux, 1993; Espiritu, 1994; Jones, 1997; Jones and McEwen, 2000);
- representing the negotiation between inside and outside worlds (neither purely inside or outside, but happening in the spaces in between) (e.g., Jones, 1997);
- continuously fluid and dynamic (not a destination) (e.g., Deaux, 1993);
- permeated and shaped by issues of privilege and power (e.g., Deaux, 1993; Espiritu, 1994; Reynolds and Pope, 1991);
- often multiple rather than singular (e.g., Loiacano, 1989; Robinson, 1993; Root, 1990);

- often representing an "awakening" process in which difference is experienced and identity is given psychological weight (e.g., Deaux, 1993; Jones, 1997). [Raetz and Lease, 2002, unpublished]

Robinson and Howard-Hamilton (2000) provide a convincing argument for considering the convergence of various identity components to better understand how to work with clients in counseling situations. They state that the convergence "(joining, meeting, merging, intersections) of race, ethnicity, gender, and other identities in person's lives" is important to understanding the experience and perspective of individuals we encounter (p. iv). They go on to say that "each of these primary identity constructs is crucial to a person's emotional and psychological development. Each intersects with other human dimensions. These intersecting variables have received limited attention . . . " (p. iv). The same argument Robinson and Howard-Hamilton make related to how counselors work with clients should also be made for those working with students on college campuses.

Sue and Sue (2003) provide a framework for understanding the multiple dimensions of identity development. Their tripartite development of personal identity model is viewed as three concentric circles. At the core is the individual with his or her unique characteristics and experiences. The outer ring of the model is more universal—our humanness. It includes common biological and physical experiences and the ability to engage in self-awareness. The second ring, and the focus of this chapter, is made up of group experiences of life, including race, ethnicity, gender, age, geographic location, and sexual orientation, to name but a few. Rather than viewing our personal development in these groups operating in isolation, Sue and Sue's model views them as salient features.

Integrating Multiple Layers of Identity Development

Research on multiple identity development is a relatively new area of inquiry. The early studies sought primarily to bring about a better understanding of how a person of color develops a sense of his or her racial and ethnic identity along with their identity as a male or female or a sexual orientation identity (for example, Chan, 1989; Espin, 1987a; Espin, 1987b; Icard, 1985–86; Loiacano, 1989). These researchers have pointed out the complexity of this process and the challenge this developmental procedure places on those working with students in higher education.

McEwen (1996), writing about the multiple identity development process, notes seven dimensions of identity that she describes as facets of a unified self rather than independent constructs: race, sexual orientation, social class, abilities and disabilities, gender, religion, and geographic region. McEwen suggests that researchers and practitioners should view identity development as social constructions and be aware that our views may be cross sections that outline all or most aspects of a person's identity, with no attention paid to patterns over time.

Jones (1997) explored multiple dimensions of identity development in female college students; many of the aforementioned themes are found in her work. The findings were ultimately expressed as a model that is, ostensibly, applicable to all students (Jones and McEwen, 2000). Jones (1997) described the multiple dimensions of identity development and difference among ten diverse women college students. Data analysis using grounded theory methodology identified ten themes that, when combined, described a core category: the contextual influences on the construction of identity. Jones and McEwen (2000) hypothesized a cohesive nucleus, which is one's sense of self. The core identity, as conceptualized by Jones (1997):

> . . . incorporated valued personal attributes and characteristics. [It] reflected what the women [participants] . . . described as their inner identities, more complex, personally defined, and less susceptible to outside influence. [It] was surrounded and overlapped by significant contextual influences that were variously constructed and understood, such as race, gender, culture, religion, and sexual orientation. Participants perceived these contexts as both externally imposed and internally defined, as well as intersecting with other dimensions of identity. Certain dimensions . . . were privileged and taken for granted; others were intensely experienced. The prominence

or salience of various identity dimensions for the individual inter-
acted with both privilege and difference [pp. 383–384].

Jones's research (1997) identified ten aspects that influence our core sense
of identity:

1. *Relative salience of identity dimensions in relation to difference.* "The experience of difference . . . exposed dimensions of identity that otherwise might
   have gone unexamined. . . . Both invisible and visible difference[s] influenced identity" (p. 379). The experience of difference and the intensity
   with which it was felt was a key factor in shaping identity, causing that
   aspect to have more importance or relevance than others. Frable (1993)
   added to this thought, noting that with invisible differences such as sexual
   orientation, individuals were more likely to feel different from the dominant group than those with more visible differences, such as race.
2. *The multiple influences of race on identity.* White women experienced
   race as salient only in specific situations, such as a racial conflict. For
   women who identified primarily with their culture, however, race formed
   part of that association but was not a dominant factor. For other women
   of color, primarily American-born African Americans, race was a primary
   part of their daily existence.
3. *Identity as a layered construction.* Identity is an evolving process, involving
   negotiation between the inner and outer worlds.
4. *The interaction of gender with other dimensions.* Gender was commonly
   experienced as important by all participants but was experienced somewhat
   differently depending on other racial and cultural factors. Some ethnic cultures prescribe certain roles for women that are more restrictive than those
   designated for men; consequently, girls and women who immigrate to the
   more egalitarian United States often identify as American more readily
   because of the increased freedom such identification offers them.
5. *The importance of cultural identifications and cultural values.* This aspect
   took on varying degrees of importance for the women in the study.
   Of those who did identify with a particular culture, however, that culture
   served a critical role in their sense of self.

6. *The influence of family and background experiences.*

7. *The role of current experiences and situational factors.*

8. *Relational inclusive values and personal beliefs.* Many participants, perhaps unlike many college students, described themselves as "activists whose work was guided by a belief in justice, fairness, and celebration of diversity" (p. 382). These values influenced their self-understandings and their worldviews.

9. *Career decisions and future planning.* Participants anticipated further changes in their identities as their careers and futures unfolded.

10. *The search for identity.* Identity was conceptualized by the participants as a fluid process, not an endpoint or destination.

It is clear that identity development and all its many facets is a complex, ongoing, and fluid process that influences and affects many aspects of our daily life.

Deaux (1993) also discussed pertinent aspects of multiple identity development, reiterating many of the previously mentioned themes. She analyzed identity as a grouping of social categories in which an individual claims membership, as well as the personal meaning associated with those categories. Her theory, similar to Cross's model (1987), proposed that identity be viewed in two ways. Social identity refers to "those roles or membership categories that a person claims as representative" (Asian American or mother); personal identity refers to "those traits and behaviors that the person finds self-descriptive, characteristics that are typically linked to one or more of the identity categories (curious and loyal)" (Deaux, 1993, p. 6). Deaux discusses social identity theory and psychological needs as explanation of identity salience. Further, she outlines three key issues for future research:

> **It is clear that identity development and all its many facets is a complex, ongoing, and fluid process that influences and affects many aspects of our daily life.**

The structure and interrelationships among multiple identities. This aspect examines salience of identities, implying a hierarchy or other structure that heightens certain identities, making them more conscious than others. This idea is similar to Reynolds and Pope's assertion (1991) and Root's assertions (1990) about aspects of identity that are assigned "other" status and that have been socially oppressed. When the individual experiences this otherness, that identity acquires salience and becomes conscious and important.

The several functions that identities serve. This issue mainly refers to the literature surrounding the concept of social identity, which advances the idea that everyone forms his identity in a social context through group membership and that those memberships happen so that various needs can be met: self-esteem, self-knowledge, and so on.

The importance of context to the development and enactment of identities. In other words, context plays a strong moderating role in identity. We must actively work to rethink what our identities mean in new contexts. For example, African American group membership may possess a specific meaning for a college student who attends a historically black college or university, while it may hold a different connotation for that same student if he or she attended a predominantly white institution. This finding is reiterated in later research, such as Johnson's work (1997) with identity development of African American college students. Finally, Deaux hypothesizes a relatively stable, coherent internal identity that undergoes a series of fluctuations or modifications, depending on situation, context, and experience. Unfortunately, it can also mean that along with multiple identities and the richness they can bring to a person, it also puts them in the position of facing discrimination and prejudice on multiple levels (Atkinson and Hackett, 1998).

Sexual Orientation Identity Formation

In addition to the previous discussions of racial and ethnic identity development, some attention should be given to the development of sexual orientation identity and gender identity. These two constructs add a different dimension to the discussion but are nonetheless important aspects of understanding the multiple layers of identity development.

Cass's social psychological model of gay/lesbian identity development (1979, 1984) assumes that sexual identity development is a process not unlike the identity development processes described earlier in this text. The model includes six stages that are both cognitive and affective components where individuals must be able to consider their behaviors and make decisions about life choices as well as consider how those choices feel. The model, like other developmental stage models such as Erikson's, considers that stages can be completed successfully, providing individuals strengths as they move to the next stage, or unsuccessfully, creating a sense of frustration or foreclosure.

Stage 1 of the model (*identity confusion*) starts at the point where a person is first aware that he/she has same-sex thoughts, sensations, or attractions. Because our society still does not consider these realizations to be a normal part of growing up, these feelings and cognitions may be frightening and anxiety provoking. At this point in the development, one would not identify him or herself as homosexual; there is only an awareness that information regarding gay, lesbian, or bisexual (GLB) issues is of interest and may impact him or her personally. Berzon (1988) suggested that at this point, the individual follow one of the following strategies:

1. *Inhibition*—This person takes in the information and senses it may apply but puts up barriers to more information, becomes celibate in hopes that the feelings will go away, or channels the feelings into actions that are antigay (internalized homophobia).
2. *Personal innocence*—Using this strategy, men may continue to engage in homosexual activity but will ensure that no emotion is attached to the behavior. On the other hand, women using this strategy would have deeply emotional relationships but guard against any physical involvement or, if physical behavior occurs, would define it as only "experimenting."
3. *Information seeking*—Using this strategy leads to movement toward the second stage of Cass's model through the adoption of a positive view of self in gathering information to assist in the beginning of a gay identity.

Identity comparison is the second stage in the model and involves developing a capacity to manage feelings about being GLB and feeling different from friends, family, and other important people in one's life. Individuals in this stage begin to see that their sexual identity may impact a number of aspects in their life (for example, career or family) and may experience a sense of loss over changing life plans.

The third stage of the model, *identity tolerance,* occurs when a person acknowledges that he or she is most likely GLB and begins to actually seek out other members of the community. It is not uncommon for some individuals at this stage to still see this identity as temporary. Once past this point, the fourth stage, *identity acceptance,* can occur. In this stage, positive interactions with other GLB individuals begin to occur more frequently. Also in this stage, individuals begin to feel more comfortable in their identity and may begin to share that information with peers and family.

Identity pride is the fifth stage. Here, individuals may actually separate themselves from interaction with heterosexuals, immerse themselves in GLB culture, friends, and organizations, and take on an activist role to varying degrees. If individuals now experience negative reactions from loved ones, foreclosure can take place.

Finally, *identity synthesis* occurs, and the individual melds the homosexual experiences with the heterosexual world in which he or she lives and works. A congruence of actions and words occurs. Once it happens, one's identity as a gay, lesbian, or bisexual person can become an integrated aspect of self—a vital part of integrating the multiple identities any individual will possess throughout a lifetime.

More recently, two other researchers studied the development of gay, lesbian, and bisexual identity development. Troiden (1989) studied gay identity development and conceived a four-stage model that he introduced in 1989. This model is not a linear process but a series of movements "back-and-forth, up-and-down" (p. 47). Like so many identity development models, this one begins with the stage of *realization* that a person is not part of and is in some way different from the majority population. A period of *identity confusion* occurs when this sense of being different is associated with perhaps being a homosexual. From this stage comes *identity assumption* when homosexual identity becomes clearer emotionally, psychologically, and behaviorally. Finally, *commitment,* or complete self-acceptance emerges with all the personal and societal issues in full realization. A sense of pride in self can now develop.

D'Augelli (1994) believed that developing an identity is a process and therefore would not refer to them as "stages." The six processes are (1) exiting heterosexual identity, (2) developing a personal lesbian/gay/bisexual identity status, (3) developing a lesbian/gay/bisexual social identity, (4) becoming a lesbian/gay/bisexual offspring, (5) developing a lesbian/gay/bisexual intimacy status, and (6) entering a lesbian/gay/bisexual community. The fact remains that sexual orientation is invisible, and the societal reaction to homosexuality creates special barriers for individuals to develop a positive gay, lesbian, or bisexual identity (Evans, Forney, and Guido-DiBrito, 1998).

Several published studies explore the multiple identity issues created for gay, lesbian, and bisexual individuals: sexual minority men and women (Fassinger and Miller, 1996; McCarn and Fassinger, 1996), black gay men and lesbians (Loiacano, 1989), Latina lesbians (Espin, 1987a), and Asian Americans (Chan, 1989). In addition, researchers are beginning to look at ways to assess gay identity (Mohr and Fassinger, 2000). Finally, more work is also needed related to college students and the impact of environmental influences on gay, lesbian, and bisexual identity formation.

Women and Gender Identity

We begin to develop a sense of ourselves as male or female in society very early in life. Josselson (1987) provided a model of identity development of women that has been used for some time to explain the path most women take to a differentiated sense of self. In her recent study, Josselson (1992) interviewed both men and woman to gain a better understanding of the continuation of identity development in the context of healthy relationships starting in the postcollege years through midlife.

Some authors have argued that the process of identity development for women is similar to the racial and ethnic identity development process (Helms, 1990). Using a four-stage model to explain this phenomenon, Helms (1990) outlines the developmental process (similar in title and task to Cross's model [1971] of racial identity development) in the attainment of a womanist identity. Women begin their identity development during the *preencounter* stage, where "the woman conforms to societal views about gender, holds a constricted view of women's roles, and nonconsciously thinks and behaves in ways that devalue women and esteem men as reference group" (Ossana, Helms, and Leonard, 1992, p. 403). The second stage, *encounter,* begins when a woman starts to question the status quo and seek alternative information about what it may mean for her to be a female in society. Using the information she takes in during this stage begins the movement to the third stage, *immersion-emersion.* Here, women search for a new definition of womanhood to create a positive sense of self. Finally, the last stage, *internalization,* occurs when women "refuse to be bound by external definitions of womanhood" (p. 403). These stages explain the journey taken by a woman to create a sense of who she is as a female in relationship to others in her family, circle of friends, and community.

McNamera and Rickard (1998) based their recent theory of feminist identity development on Cross's work (1971). The five-stage model provides a framework for understanding how women move from a sense of men as clearly superior to females to a more relativistic view of life as a female and a desire to be involved in social action to bring about change in the lives of other women. Between these two extremes, women must develop a conscious understanding of prejudice and oppression, engage in a heightened sense of anger over the inequities, and seek ways to team with other women as comrades.

A recent study conducted to explore this type of development in a college-age population (Ossana, Helms, and Leonard, 1992) examined the relationship of womanist attitudes and college women's self-esteem to their perceptions of the campus environment. They found support for Helms's theoretical framework, finding that there was a positive relationship between self-esteem and *internalization* and a negative relationship between self-esteem and the *encounter* stage. They also found a negative relationship between the year in college and perception of gender bias in the environment. These findings show that underclass women who are more likely to be in an earlier stage of developing their womanist identity may view themselves as "less than" their male counterparts. Further research is needed in this area to assist those working with college-age women to provide a safe, supportive environment where they can further explore these important developmental issues.

After a number of years, there seems to be a resurgence of research on women's identity development. There can be no doubt that more is needed, particularly to explore the role of being a female as well as a member of other social, political, ethnic, and cultural groups. Peterson's qualitative study (2000) of Caucasian women's and African American women's identity development across the lifespan is one example of the direction this research needs to take in the future.

Implications

The multiple dimensions of identity create multiple radio stations covering the myriad of issues and developmental factors important to understand. These additional theories of identity are provided to help highlight the station that may be needed on the radio at any one particular time. As individual students find their own way, educators should understand some of the complex developmental issues involved in creating an identity. Today's students are more diverse, older, and more likely to carry these multiple dimensions of identity. It is up to educators to stay abreast of the developmental theories that can help us understand our diverse students.

Educators should understand some of the complex developmental issues involved in creating an identity.

Integration of Identity Development Theory into Practice

A NEW MOOD IN THE TWENTY-FIRST CENTURY is apparent regarding racial issues mediated by three postmodern trends: (1) the increasing opposition to civil rights–era laws that provided equity and access for African American college students; (2) the resonant demands from Asian American, Latino, and Latina students, the fastest-growing populations, for increased multiethnic institutional changes; and (3) "the changing racial ideologies that college students from distinct ethnic backgrounds bring to increasingly diverse campus communities" (Bowman and Smith, 2002, p. 103). These trends will be present in our college environments for many years to come. The question for faculty and administrators is how present practices should be changed to address and accommodate these trends.

These trends will only continue the need to have dialogue about differences. The focus of this monograph has been on providing information that can help faculty and administrators understand diverse students to promote constructive dialogue about difficult issues. This chapter applies the knowledge gained about how diverse students' identities develop to creating a better environment for all students.

The manner in which the previous theories can impact the work of faculty and administrators in higher education depends on individuals' willingness to shift their own perspective to include those from diverse backgrounds. This chapter focuses on offering ideas to those who are willing to make this shift and find the "courage for social change" (Tatum, 1997, p. 203). The first section discusses the need to understand the campus culture from both administrators' and students' perspective, as it is the campus culture that often determines the behavior of students. The second section addresses implications for administrators and the third implications for faculty. These two categories are separated because administrators and faculty interact with students in different contexts. To change the present system that discourages students takes courage to speak out and invite dialogue about these emotional issues.

Campus Culture

Students on college campuses who experience a system of oppression every day have tremendous difficulty maintaining good grades, communicating with classmates, connecting with faculty, and feeling comfortable calling their future alma mater "home." These issues become the survival behaviors they focus on that can in turn delay other developmental issues (Taub and McEwen, 1992). It is clear that on a daily basis, life on college and university campuses is "structured in terms of historical and collective memories, as well as in terms of racialized places and interaction" (Feagin, Vera, and Imani, 1996, p. 84).

Students on college campuses who experience a system of oppression every day have tremendous difficulty maintaining good grades, communicating with classmates, connecting with faculty, and feeling comfortable calling their future alma mater "home."

The campus environment is largely determined by the collective characteristics of the inhabitants (Strange and Banning, 2001). The first aspect that should be understood about campus culture is that "dominant campus features reflect the influence of the dominant groups" (p. 122). As a result, the culture reflected on predominantly white institutions is one of the white majority; regardless of how many diversity statements are published, the campus environment continues to reflect the dominant group. This component of campus culture can influence how the racial, ethnic, or multiple identities of students develop. If students of color perceive that their race is not valued, their struggle to define themselves racially can be further heightened by this inhospitable environment. The challenge then becomes how to make the majority culture inclusive and welcoming of all the diverse cultures present on campus.

The first recommendation to create a more diverse environment is often to increase the structural diversity in the student and faculty bodies (Hurtado, Milem, Clayton-Pedersen, and Allen, 1999). The presence of diverse students, faculty, and staff can promote more contact, interaction, and involvement with people who are different and can challenge the present dominant paradigm. This challenge promotes a learning environment that is respectful of diversity and expands one's view of how the world functions (Hurtado, Milem, Clayton-Pedersen, and Allen, 1999). Monocultural environments, which provide exposure to only one culture, are not as effective in helping students learn how to deal with different views, opinions, and work styles.

A second recommendation is to assess the complex responses needed to address issues of inclusion on a particular campus (Strange and Banning, 2001). Campus assessments should include a review of existing, representative documents to determine whether only one culture is being advocated. This type of assessment often requires consideration of new assessment tools. Providing a group of students with cameras to do a photographic assessment (Strange and Banning, 2001) can provide administrators with interesting information on how messages are interpreted and what values students see on the campus. Simply asking students to point out or define images that define the campus can provide insight into how the institutional culture is portrayed to students. These more informal techniques can often provide a more accurate picture than the formal surveys of how the nuances in the campus culture are interpreted. Though overt images are easier to identify, the nuances can also contribute to a positive or negative environment for diverse populations. Changing the campus culture to be more inclusive requires an organizational approach to diversity. Institutions should consider comprehensive approaches to deal with the number of special needs that will come with the increase in diversity (Smith, 1996).

What these two recommendations have in common is the need to assess and deliberately identify how the campus culture can be changed to be more inclusive of the diverse identities on campus. Those in the majority culture will assume that the campus is inviting because it reflects their dominant culture. For this reason, a different lens is needed to truly assess and identify what the campus culture is and how it can influence diverse students.

To tailor recommendations to educators, the next section deals specifically with implications for administrators and faculty. Each group provides a different level of support to diverse students, and therefore each section is treated separately.

Implications for Administrators

Administrators have two major responsibilities that influence the learning environment for diverse populations. First, they are more likely to create the policies that govern behavior. And second, they are the ones that enforce those policies. (By policies, we mean all policies that can pertain to students, or staff, or faculty.) It is administrators who determine how the mission of the institution is carried out and thus influence how inclusive the environment can feel for many groups of people. Though there are many issues to consider if an administrator wants to create an inclusive environment, this section concentrates on two concerns: (1) level of involvement diverse people are given and (2) the ability to express cultural identity within the environment.

Involving Diverse People in Decision Making

Institutional responses to public policies are not always clear (Callahan, 1994). A major responsibility of administrators is to create the campus response to public policies by formulating the institutional policy that will guide behavior on their particular campus. The importance of this responsibility in the context of creating an inclusive environment is not always considered.

Perhaps the most visible type of policies that can influence diverse faculty and staff are the policies governing gateways to the institution. For faculty and staff, the gateway to an institution is through hiring practices. These practices in turn affect students, because they are the ones who seek out these individuals during their academic experience. A policy or practice that may seem fair to the majority may actually hurt the institution by not infusing the new diversity of employees an institution needs to meet the needs of the increasingly diverse student body. For example, several colleges have systems that award positions based on seniority rather than on the needs of the institution. In these situations, the person with seniority may not have the skills necessary to deal with the multicultural environment the college is seeking to promote. As a result, the person placed in the position does not reflect the desired mission of the institution and may feel frustrated because he or she prefers a monocultural environment rather than the multicultural environment the institution has or is seeking. The conflicts and unwelcoming behaviors someone with this sentiment can create in an administrative position are often felt, yet few understand the relationship between this behavior and the need to review institutional policies. Students of color often informally communicate with each other about which offices are truly welcoming and which ones are not. No office or program should ever be seen as unwelcoming for any student. Administrators are assigned the duty of having the big picture and therefore they must also understand how policies reinforcing the status quo may actually be hurting the diversity of students they are seeking to attract as well as the success of those students.

One way to address this issue is to involve diverse individuals in policy formulation or revision or the development of "new approaches to policy and organizations" (Smith, 1996, p. 538). This process should include faculty, staff, and students; all three levels are affected by institutional policies in different ways. Few institutions engage in systematic review of existing policies. If an academic or student policy is routinely appealed or circumvented, it is likely that the policy does not respond to the present needs of the institution. Yet most institutions continue to create appeal boards rather than take on the task of policy review. Systematic review of a policy can promote a revision that is more effective and inclusive of the diversity reflected in the environment. This review should also include a clarification of institutional values and the connection of those values to the institution's mission (Smith, 1996). In considering both values and mission, administrators can reflect on the policy impacts on the environment and whose values have been in place to this point.

Most institutions continue to create appeal boards rather than take on the task of policy review.

The key to these recommendations is that the administrator has a sense of their identity and how that identity impacts their perceptions of the campus culture. With a new lens, administrators should work to view how things work from multiple perspectives. This shift in paradigm can make a difference in creating an environment that values diversity.

Expressions of Cultural Identity

The other responsibility that falls on the shoulders of administrators is to regulate how the environment is interpreted. This regulation is maintained by policies and procedures that determine what is exhibited and how the institution is portrayed to the outside world. Earlier, we discussed photographs that describe how the institution is interpreted. If all or most of the pictures portray the majority culture, how many administrators would see it as a problem? Few would actually consider the fact that there are no expressions of the diverse cultural identities on the campus as a problem, yet it sends out messages to students from those cultures not represented. Expressions of culture can be seen in artwork, signs, programs being promoted, or in structural representation.

For all diverse groups to feel included, expressions of their own cultural identity—not just the expressions of the majority culture—should be seen on the campus. Because the majority is just that—the majority—they may not realize how prevalent their culture is articulated and how little diversity is expressed, which is how privilege is maintained for those in the majority culture. The notion that everyone should just "fit in" is one entrenched in assimilation rather than respect for diversity. Administrators often regulate how culture is expressed through policies on academic offerings, postings, office use, and common art spaces. It is important to consider the message that is being sent by all these policies and to consider them as a whole rather than only as individual circumstances, which are then explained away as unique issues and not the norm.

Recommendations for Administrators

The first recommendation for administrators is to educate themselves about the issues of diverse students and the environment they perceive in their own institution. For this education process to succeed, administrators must first recognize their own biases and privileges and be open to different interpretations.

This monograph is the first step in this educational process. The ability to see things from a different perspective is perhaps the most useful tool an administrator can possess when dealing with students of color. It is easier to explain away the complaints with jargon about how difficult it is to please everyone. Rather than taking this approach, administrators must consider benefits from the status quo of a particular program or policy. Reflection from a different perspective may be surprising and force administrators to consider various viewpoints instead of only the majority perspective.

The second recommendation is to review everyday things. Often, administrators take for granted that everyone has the same level of understanding they do and therefore use lingo and explanations that do not truly address the needs of diverse students. It is not unusual for a first-generation college student who has completed orientation to not understand what the process for declaring a major is about. They are not sure what a "major" is, much less why they should, or need to, declare one. Diverse students *may* not have the tools and knowledge necessary to jump in and be part of the community. They may need more guidance and assistance. Administrators are in a position to help students create cognitive road maps for how to manage the college experience. It should not be assumed that all students get help and advice from parents. Often, parents who are from different cultures do not know how to support or advise their children on college issues. It is not that they do not want to support their child; it is that they do not know what to expect or how they can support the educational process. Parents can influence both the identity of the student and the adjustment process in college. The key is to make the environment inclusive enough for students to (1) understand what information they need, even if they do not realize it, (2) easily find the help they need, and (3) see themselves reflected in the environment in such a way that their identity is valued and they feel comfortable asking for help.

The final recommendation for administrators is to purposefully create spaces and programs that reflect diverse cultures. These spaces can help diverse students feel comfortable expressing or searching for their identity. This process of creating purposeful spaces should be done throughout the campus, not just in the one area where minority students are expected to hang out. Instead, the goal should be to expose majority students to diverse cultures. This exposure will help create an inclusive environment and promote student learning by opening discussions that were not previously happening. The goal of creating an inclusive campus is difficult and requires cooperation from all levels, and the key to making it happen for those involved is to see how their own experiences and identities are enhanced by the diversity found on the college campus.

Implications for Faculty Members

Making a paradigm shift is difficult for faculty, particularly if they are asked to modify teaching techniques and classroom material to be more inclusive of underrepresented groups. It is even more difficult when the faculty members have been taught, overtly and covertly, that the traditional westernized method of teaching or "banker's education" (Freire, 1987, p. 71) is the best one. Many faculty may not see the need to make the paradigm shift because of the paucity of diverse students in the college classroom. A faculty member from a dominant group may ask why it is necessary to change his or her method of teaching to be more inclusive when he or she teaches mostly students who look like him or her. This question can be further examined when faculty members are asked to reflect on their experiences as learners. How many faculty of color or women taught them during their college career? Did they have primarily white male faculty during their college career? Did they have a faculty member of color or woman who taught from the framework of an inclusive learning environment? In most cases, faculty in today's classrooms learned and honed their teaching techniques and styles based on white male models from their undergraduate and graduate classes. Even though the demographic trends clearly indicate an increase in the number of Latinos, Latinas, Asian Americans, and African Americans, the individuals who can impact social change (faculty) are not acknowledging, recognizing, or empowering oppressed groups. Faculty, more than any other group on campus, are in the position to affect the success of diverse students. Additionally, faculty are not challenging students from the dominant culture to be aware of their privilege and therefore perpetuate obliviousness of other cultural groups. "Among educators there has to be an acknowledgement that any effort to transform institutions so that they reflect a multicultural standpoint must take into consideration the fears teachers have when asked to shift their paradigms" (hooks, 1994, p. 36).

Understanding Identity Development

When faculty redesign their courses to become more inclusive by bringing diverse perspectives into the classroom as well as the content of the material, the process may generate a range of emotional responses from students (Tatum, 1996). These behavioral reactions may range from complete detachment from the class stemming from anger and resentment to excitement and eagerness because lost voices are finally being heard. Tatum noted in her experience teaching courses on racism for more than twenty years that if the instructor does not address the emotional dissonance exhibited in class, some cognitive interference will occur, resulting in a lack of mastery and understanding of the material being taught.

Infusing diversity issues into the course content may create a tremendous amount of dissonance for students and instructors, which is why an understanding of identity development is critical. Faculty should have a strong sense of personal racial, ethnic, and multicultural identity development to comfortably guide students through their own awareness of privilege, oppression, and racial consciousness. If faculty do not have a sense of their own power and privilege in the classroom, the hidden curriculum is unknowingly perpetuated (Jones and Young, 1997). The hidden curriculum works, covertly, toward "power relationships, cultural hegemony, and political relationships" (p. 93). This classroom dynamic hinders the cognitive and psychosocial identity development of girls, women, and people of color in particular. Helms discusses the importance of those in positions of power and privilege unlearning their prejudicial behavior or abandoning racism and developing a nonracist white identity (Helms and Cook, 1999; Helms, 2000). Again, racial identity development is as important for the faculty member as it is for the student to unravel and deconstruct.

Similar to the teaching experiences Tatum discusses, Howard-Hamilton and Hinton (2002) examined the behavioral patterns of student's voices through monitoring journal narratives and personal interactions in a course entitled Diverse College Students. Additionally, they collected qualitative data on the behavioral, emotional, and cognitive patterns exhibited by students in their classrooms and workshops for more than twenty years. Howard-Hamilton and Hinton (2002) developed the behavioral patterns of multicultural competence model (see Figure 1, page 34). It is cyclical and presumes that those persons responding to the content and information learned while studying racial, ethnic, and diversity issues will move through the cycle continuously throughout life. The breaks in the cycle allow for periods of reflection, renewal, and preparation to encounter the next behavioral pattern.

The five behavioral patterns of multicultural competence are defined below and connected with excerpts of student narratives and dialogue that emerged when analyzing their journals:

Anticipatory anxiousness/anxiety—Students exhibited a sense of positive anxiousness or normal anxiety, wanting to delve into the topics planned for the semester and learn more about themselves as well as other multicultural groups. There were also some students who were not excited about the course or the content; they exhibited a tremendous amount of anxiety about how others viewed their culture. Some feelings of anxiousness were excitement, hopefulness, joy, and openness. Other feelings of anxiety were anger, frustration, fear, guilt, and shame. Faculty should not ignore feelings of anxiety and anxiousness because they are potential sources of growth and development if challenged appropriately. According to Corey (2001, p. 152), "anxiety is associated with the excitement accompanying the birth of a new idea. Thus, we experience anxiety when we use our freedom to move out of the known into the realm of the unknown." Several student quotes capture the essence of this pattern:

> *During class I became excited by the upcoming content of the course. I need to confront any problems or hesitations I have regarding speaking about diversity openly and areas that I have little knowledge or experience with. I appreciate the opportunity to be able to grow in this capacity with a group of diverse peers. . . . I look forward to continually expanding my use of a "multicultural lens" to improve my interactions with others and my perceiving of encountered multicultural issues.*

> *I am not sure about this class. I don't think I've ever been in a class where I felt the content was detrimental to my life. . . . I hold diversity close to my heart; however, when my beliefs are challenged, I feel I struggle to back them up. I want to be armed with knowledge!*
>
> *I'm not sure what to expect out of this class. I know that I have a lot to learn about different minority populations and about my own perceptions of those populations [that] may be incorrect.*
>
> *This class should be interesting. I am not sure about spending a whole semester discussing diversity topics, but it should turn out alright.*

Curiosity about the acquisition of knowledge—Students are shocked and appalled when they discover that there is so much more to learn about the history of diverse groups and that their current level of education is woefully inadequate. They want to read and learn more about the history of culturally diverse people, and they realize that what they were taught in elementary and secondary school may have been written to favor privileged groups. Students noted that the reading materials have begun to challenge what they had formerly considered to be historical truths:

> *The reading for today sort of irritated me and also opened my eyes. The guy was talking about how he was having a discussion with his White friend and that friend insisted that he understood discrimination and prejudice. However, the author believed that he had a better, more operative understanding than the White man. In fact, he went on to say that Whites say that they understand discrimination as a form of denial of injustices. What a crock of shit! I understand discrimination because I have seen it. I have been a victim once or twice, but more often than not I have seen discrimination imposed on someone else. I suppose the author is right that I do not understand what that particular person feels at that particular time, but then again no one does. But for him to say that I cannot or will not ever be able to understand discrimination or exclusion is absurd. What is the point?*

I don't want to be American anymore. I think that this class is going to be very depressing. We watched the video in class today about oppression in America. Watching the history of oppression, hatred, and violence in America is difficult and makes it hard to be proud to be an American. It's no wonder they don't teach the true history of America in grammar school. They can't. It is rated R. I feel really ignorant about historical facts and oppression in our country; I feel like I might offend people around every corner with every discussion. And NOT EVEN KNOW IT. How sad. I don't even know the people around me.

I thought I might experiment with racism today. I was going to list each racist comment I heard. Ever really listened? Here are my totals: Race/ethnicity, 12; Class, 6; Nation, 1; Sex/gender, 2; GLBT, 18. . . . It started just as racist comments but quickly expanded just walking across campus, in the union, etc. I heard the previous horrifying number of comments.

Epiphany/acceptance/privileged status—Students realize that they have been the benefactors of unearned privileges. This realization pertains to people of color who are from a high socioeconomic status, women, and men from the dominant culture. White heterosexual males are not the only persons who have unearned privileges; however, they do note that there are varying degrees of privilege that give some more power than others. The students' comments indicate that a new view of cultural concession has been awakened.

As a White female, I feel little discrimination and I am afforded most, if not all, the privileges of White males. I rarely wonder about the looks given me on the street, where I can walk and park, why someone is uneasy around me (generally it's just because they don't like me and not because they don't like me because I am a White female). I can see people like me in the cafeteria, stores, movies. . . . I recognize this. I haven't always but I do now.

When I was interviewing the Asian international students for my action plan, I realized something. I have a certain racism towards non-White people due to fear. I think that this is a fear based largely on my pride. This fear is a fear that I won't understand, that my ignorance about language, culture, or world events will come to light. As I stepped out of my comfort zone to meet with not one but two international students, I began to question why I don't have more interactions with students similar to them. I thought about how I have little patience or free time to try to understand someone who struggles with language. . . . As I was meeting with the students, I was surprised to understand how easily my privilege allows me to ignore those around me who are different and not only perpetuates racism but also stands in my way of becoming an effective professional.

Comfort with oneself and others—Individuals have a sense of peace with who they are as racial/ethnic individuals. Multicultural differences exist, and everyone has a meaningful story. One student described her own experience with this process and the importance of respect and understanding to promote cultural competence:

I think so many times that when we talk about diversity, people think that you have to know what it is like to be someone else to understand them. Yes, that would help but I cannot change my race or gender; therefore, I will never know what it is like to be anyone but me. All that I can do is appreciate who I am, and be respectful of those who are different [from] me. It is not about trying to feel every feeling that someone else feels or saying I completely understand because you know that I will never know what it is like to be discriminated against because of my race. . . . We just have to understand that people feel and react the way they do for a reason, [and that] there is always history behind everyone's actions!!!

Multicultural competence as a lifelong process—A sense of social consciousness and personal passion must be present to continue the fight against oppression. Students need to maintain a level of normal anxiety, be willing to connect with others not like themselves, and increase their knowledge base. They are also charged with being responsible citizens and challenging those who perpetuate oppression in our society. Two students share their anxiety about becoming promoters of social justice:

> *I don't know if I am ready for this responsibility. The responsibility of changing society. I am scared that it will be hard. And that people will not be receptive. And that it is a sensitive issue. And race is a heated, emotional topic. Because there are millions who live within the bounds of their racial identities everyday. The concern I have is that there are millions of privileged idiots leading their happy lives everyday without an idea of why this issue might be important to them.*

> *Diversity Poem*
> *I am ignorant. Please don't be angry with me.*
> *I am White. Please don't be angry with me.*
> *I see an understanding of your perspective. Please don't be angry with me.*
> *I want to know you. Please don't be angry with me.*
> *I want to learn history. Please don't be angry with me.*
> *I want to learn your stories. Please don't be angry with me.*
> *I want you to feel accepted. Please don't be angry with me.*
> *I want to be accepted. Please don't be angry with me.*

Understanding identity development will help faculty design and implement teaching strategies that may enhance the learning environment for all students.

Based on the comments made in the students' narratives about understanding racial identity development, it is clear that faculty should understand the stages of white racial consciousness as well as other identity models. Understanding identity development will help faculty design and implement teaching strategies that may enhance the learning environment for all students.

How Culture Influences the Classroom Experience

Persons from oppressed cultures tend to live in a world that does not value them, marginalizes their efforts, erases their history, and silences their voices. Dominant cultures have an opportunity to see themselves reflected in textbooks, the media, and models in the classroom in the role of professors, administrators, and trustees. They become the ones who shape the classroom experience by sharing information that is familiar to their frame of reference and negating (overtly or covertly) the experiences of others. Collusion with faculty occurs because they have experiences similar to the students in the classroom who look like them. Unfamiliar topics make the dominant group uncomfortable, and they resist hearing anything that may challenge, change, or transform the information that is being discussed. When talking about race or racism, students from the dominant culture become radically resistant, and they (1) attempt to ban the topic from the classroom, especially in racially diverse settings; (2) attempt to convince the class that America is a just society and everyone is equal; and (3) project prejudicial behaviors on others, failing to recognize the impact of oppression and racism on their own lives (Tatum, 1992).

Therefore, the dominant culture's ideologies, philosophies, and artifacts prevail in every thread of the campus fabric. One philosophy of the dominant culture is that students from oppressed groups gain admission to college because of affirmative action, because their grades, test scores, or rank in high school did not merit consideration. Moreover, beliefs that students of color are lazy, not motivated to succeed, lack independence, and do not embrace the American ethic (you will succeed if you work hard) contribute to the oppressive attitudes felt by these students, particularly in the classroom (Bowman and Smith, 2002).

Quite simply, if students from nondominant cultures are uncomfortable and silenced in a classroom, how can they concentrate, participate, and learn? Reports from focus group interviews with black students disclosed treatment in the classroom that was discriminatory and demeaning, "including often being treated as the spokesperson for the race, being graded down for writing on African American topics, and being subjected to subtle racist joking" (Feagin, 2000, p. 170). Students also said that the courses and curricula were racially biased, and many students became so psychologically battered that they considered dropping out because of the negative racial climate. Conversely, whites believed "that they as individuals are no longer supportive of racism, while the numerous effects, old and new, of racism continue unabated. This is particularly clear in the academy, which typically sees itself as a liberal force for racial equity (Scheurich and Young, 2002). The problem is that campuses are strongly oriented toward the dominant culture and clearly resistant to major changes, even though the demographic makeup of college students is shifting radically. The faculty do not see themselves as perpetuators of racism in the academy, even though the curricula and pedagogies taught to them in their academic career reflected white racial privilege and bias that positively serve the dominant culture and oppress others (Scheurich and Young, 2002). Faculty need support designing and implementing curricular changes that will include varying cultures on college campuses. This support will be effective only if faculty are open to experiencing changes in their own paradigms. The "technical" aspects of inclusion in teaching (saying the politically correct thing or including a statement of nondiscrimination on the syllabus) do not mean an instructor understands the dynamics occurring in his or her classroom. Instead, it only illustrates the ability to follow a checklist of things to do. The process that should be supported is the reflection on and intentionality of changing the way oppression is perpetuated in teaching. It is a complex and long process that may take several interventions to make a difference.

Teaching Strategies

Faculty shoulder the responsibility of teaching and nurturing students by allowing them a place where they can come and dialogue, seek, and share knowledge without fear of biases, hindrances, and impediments (Feagin, Vera, and Imani, 1996). Numerous teaching strategies can create a learning environment that is not hostile and is inclusive. Tatum (1992, pp. 18–22) stresses the importance of reducing students' resistance before the implementation of new teaching methods through four strategies:

Creation of a safe classroom atmosphere by establishing clear guidelines for discussion. Ground rules should be clearly established at the beginning of the class stating that inappropriate statements (racist or sexist, for example) will not be tolerated. Every student has a voice and a story to share, and their individual experiences should be respected. Students should use "I" statements when referring to experiences or beliefs they speak about in class. Faculty should continually model appropriate behavior by challenging inappropriate statements and restating the class ground rules when needed.

Creation of opportunities for self-generated knowledge. When students challenge material presented in the texts or lectures, create opportunities for them to have a hands-on or immersion assignment to facilitate the power of self-generated knowledge. This approach allows them to move beyond stereotypes and preconceived beliefs based on the knowledge they acquired from a system of social oppression.

Provision of an appropriate developmental model that students can use as a framework for understanding their own process. Students will make emotional responses to the material presented in class or to the shift from a banker's education format to an inclusive classroom in a predictable manner related to the stages of racial identity development noted earlier. It may be useful to provide a lecture on racial identity development or social identity so that students can comprehend why they may be experiencing guilt or anger and how to respond to each other when statements may sound disturbing.

Exploration of strategies to empower students as change agents. It is important as educators that we prepare students for the arduous process of revealing information about themselves that may prove to be painful such as the realization that they have been the beneficiaries of privileges that they had taken for granted (McIntosh, 1988, 1998). Once this realization has occurred, however, guilt and shame can be turned into proactive revolutionary behavior. Finding models that use privilege and voice to enact change helps students realize that the struggle experienced by the oppressed is everyone's struggle. One method of encouraging students to change social oppression is reading antiracist theory written by authors such as Paulo Freire (1987), Joe Feagin (2000), and Peggy McIntosh (1988, 1989) or attending lectures by whites who are willing to share their story about how they became aware of their privileges.

Teaching techniques can increase students' cognitive ability to think beyond a dualistic (right or wrong, black or white) frame of reference and become more reflective thinkers (King, 2000) if coursework is thought provoking and challenging. It is important that students see multiple perspectives in the content of course materials they are required to read (Howard-Hamilton, 2000). This material should be supplemented with videos and guest speakers to give students an opportunity to have contact with persons from diverse groups.

Maintaining contact with all students is very important in the creation of a culturally responsive environment. As noted, many students initially experience painful emotional setbacks when discussing issues related to diversity, racism, social oppression, and privilege. Instructors should meet with students periodically about assignments or grades that could lead to other issues related to becoming culturally competent and comfortable around people different from them. Individual office meetings can be listed in the syllabus as a requirement of the course. When lecturing, instructors should make sure that gender-neutral pronouns are used or should provide examples using females as often as males. Racial examples should not be limited to African Americans or blacks and whites; when discussing cultural issues, provide examples from various racial and ethnic groups, including Asian Americans, American Indians, Latinos, and Latinas.

> **Maintaining contact with all students is very important in the creation of a culturally responsive environment.**

Academicians who believe in teaching to transcend traditional pedagogical methods have shared activities, assignments, and in-class experiences that have been effective in creating a classroom environment where learners respect each other's experiences (Baxter Magolda, 2000; Brookfield, 1995; Fries-Britt, 2000; hooks, 1994; Howard-Hamilton, 2000; Ortiz, 2000; Tatum, 1997; Wlodkowski and Ginsberg, 1995). Faculty should write an autobiography that entails their learning experiences from kindergarten through graduate school (Brookfield, 1995) and includes successful teaching methods implemented by mentors as well as challenging and nonsupportive classroom experiences. The autobiography serves as an empathy tool to remember the experiences from the student perspective.

Within the first few weeks of a new semester, students should write their personal story or autobiography and share a portion of it with their classmates. This experience gives all students a voice and cultural context that helps in framing how students feel when reacting to discussions or assignments in class. Student journals also give voice and meaning to new issues taught in class. Additionally, journals provide feedback for the faculty member on how the student is dealing with the culturally responsive curriculum. Writing assignments could also include a short reflective paper at the end of each class period so that students can note what they have learned as well as how they felt when receiving the new information.

Classes should have a dialogue component so that reflection and critical analysis can occur after the readings and lecture are completed. Students should learn how to become self-authors of their own learning by making meaning that is from their personal frame of reference. This critical-thinking process helps them move from the dualistic stance—the professor has all the knowledge, and I must memorize the facts—to becoming more reflective and understanding that not all material written by scholars is the "truth."

Case studies connecting course content to relevant experiences provide students with a realistic framework for what is being taught. Students can find the answers to the case by using their own personal experiences in combination with the material from class. Moving a step beyond the case study approach is the use of action plans or an immersion experience that moves students out of their comfort zone into an area that is unfamiliar. If a class is studying Judaism, it may be assigned to attend a service in a synagogue and speak to the rabbi. This assignment moves the student beyond intellectualizing the experiences of Jews to becoming part of that culture.

Recommendations for Faculty

If college classrooms are to become more inclusive, a starting point for the process is necessary. Institutions should create opportunities for faculty and staff to learn how to become more sensitive to diversity and multiculturally competent. One method is the development of an annual teaching and learning conference that includes sessions on strategies to improve the environment for diverse students and creative activities to promote multicultural sensitivity (Garcia and Smith, 1996). Faculty members should be provided with opportunities to share their feelings about shifting to a more inclusive manner of teaching with facilitators who have been through this process and can discuss how it was painful yet liberating and raised human consciousness (Freire, 1987). "Progressive professors working to transform the curriculum so that it does not reflect biases or reinforce systems of domination are most often the individuals willing to take the risks that engaged pedagogy requires and to make their teaching practices a site of resistance" (hooks, 1994, p. 21). Faculty members should request regular class observations by colleagues who have implemented inclusive curricular designs so that they can assist them in creating new teaching strategies.

Another method of engaging students in transformational thought and dialogue is to provide workshops on white racism facilitated by white students from higher education, student affairs, counseling, or any other human services area. Students can share their journeys of personal revelation about social oppression and racism. Tatum (1992) notes that "educating White students about race and racism changes attitudes in ways that go beyond the classroom boundaries. As White students move through their own stages of identity development, they take their friends with them by engaging them in dialogue. They share articles they have read with roommates, and involve them in their projects" (p. 22).

Finally, change can occur if the institution takes an active and participatory stance in eliminating social oppression by hiring diverse faculty in underrepresented disciplines. Administrative leaders should be from diverse groups and not only represent stereotypical groups or departments, such as multicultural affairs or women's centers. Freire (1987) found that a true movement of liberation includes action, not just intellectual or symbolic gestures; therefore, colleges and universities should provide a clear and concise mission statement that stresses the importance of creating a caring community (Garcia and Smith, 1996). Further, they should provide the support mechanisms necessary to implement the mission in the classroom and though extracurricular activities. Educators have a tremendous amount of power to engage, challenge, and support students so that they can resist traditional socially oppressive paradigms and become more fully self-actualized and feel comfortable becoming part of the struggle to fight oppression.

Conclusions and Future Implications

Promoting the success of diverse students is not an activity with a checklist; it requires intensive work and intentional behavior on the part of individual educators. We hope that the information provided here will prompt readers to question and confront situations that do not promote success for all students.

As educators become more familiar with the identity development of college students, more research should emerge on this important construct. Assuming that higher education enrollments will follow the trend of the U.S. population, then faculty and administrators must be prepared to deal with an increasingly diverse student body. All of us need to gain information about students to have an informed dialogue. If educators want to provide a supportive environment, they must first understand their students' developmental needs. Students of color want to succeed; our task is to make sure they understand the maps and options available to them. Without this information, we are creating unconscious barriers that may feel insurmountable.

Continuing the idea of higher education as a marketplace for ideas will require all of us who work in colleges to become comfortable with the difficult dialogue of diversity. Though the roots of higher education include debate and discussion, it is "not clear that dealing with conflict, particularly the kind of conflict apt to become emotional, is one that institutions can deal with very effectively" (Smith, 1996, p. 535). It is clear that trying to create diverse, pluralistic, and accepting environments will make some uncomfortable. The process of working through that discomfort is what is needed for understanding and constructive discourse. As authors, we hope that we can contribute to both the discomfort and the discourse.

Appendix A. Case Study: Defining Academic Diversity at Reflective College

Reflective College is a midsize (11,000 students), four-year, public liberal arts college that was established in 1882 originally as an all-male military institute. Although Reflective College became co-ed in the late 1950s, it took thirty years for women students to feel welcomed at Reflective. The campus is nestled in the rural community of Anywhere, U.S., which has a population of 20,000 and is located forty-five miles from the state capital.

Reflective College is located on 150 acres of land immaculately land-scaped and maintained so that there is no loss of space for students to meditate, reflect, and be spiritually connected to the environment. The campus also contains forty-nine buildings that have been restored or constructed within the past ten years and architecturally designed to parallel the older structures on campus. The most recent facility constructed is the 220,000–square foot Peace Athletics and Recreation Center. More than 65 percent of the student body actively participates in some sort of intramural or intercollegiate sports activity.

The students at Reflective College come from thirty-four states and several international countries. The student body comprises 649 men and 351 women, and 74 percent are from the town of Anywhere. The racial/ethnic composition is 2 percent African American, 2 percent Latino, and 1 percent Asian American, American Indian, and multiracial. Although there is a Multicultural Student Association on campus, its members are considered to be hand picked and pro-moted by the college administrators because they fit in. The perception is that these students do not rock the boat but maintain the status quo.

A new organization called "Students of Color at Reflective College" (SOC-R) was created by several Latino and African American students, who banded together and successfully lobbied the institution to purchase an older home near the campus or build a cultural center. Many students at Reflective College are upset that the serene physical environment may be disrupted to place an "unimportant structure" on campus. Students have begun to wage a hostile e-mail discourse on this issue, and SOC-R members are beginning to feel uncomfortable about the brutal conversations about race and who belongs at Reflective College. SOC-R members and the Multicultural Student Association have reluctantly decided to collaborate and create a course that could provide a safe place and space for a discourse on diversity. They approached the faculty council with their idea, citing one of the core values noted in the Reflective College catalogue: We strive to provide a rigorous liberal arts education and curriculum that fosters an understanding of and appreciation for other cultures. Faculty at Reflective College responded favorably, because they are dedicated to the liberal arts mission of the institution. The classroom ratio is 12/1, and a teacher is always ready to promote the growth of a Reflective College student.

A select group of faculty and students worked together to create a course that fit the values of the institution. After many reviews by the faculty curriculum committee, a new course was introduced into the general education electives that focused on social justice issues. Members of SOC-R and the Multicultural Student Association promoted the need for the course, and they continue to be active in lobbying the administration to make sure it is offered.

This new course has never been taught at the college, but an experienced professor has volunteered to take it on. Though he is white and has been at this predominantly white institution for more than twenty-five years, he feels he is in touch with the diversity of the student body and can create a good course. His teaching evaluations have always been very positive, and therefore the department chairs feels comfortable with this solution. Moreover, no additional funds would need to be spent to offer this new course. It seems like a win-win situation: Students get what they want, and no funds are needed to accomplish it.

The fall semester begins, and the new Social Justice class is offered for the first time. The first couple of weeks seem to be going well, but this week the dean has received several anonymous complaints from students. It seems that in an effort to include the students of color, the professor has had each student of color make a presentation about his or her culture and answer questions from the other students. Several students of color were offended by the questions asked by the white students, but the professor had stressed the need to learn about differences. The students were also "interrogated" about SOC-R and the need to build a cultural center on campus. Furthermore, the minority students felt they were expected to do an extra assignment, because they had to present information about their culture but white students did not.

On the other hand, the white students feel like they are being forced to accept "this diversity stuff" and that students of color do not accept their opinions. One student felt as though only the opinions of the students of color mattered and that the majority had little say on how the class should proceed. After all, white students are the majority on the campus, and those other students just need to fit in.

The faculty member has a strong reputation for bringing up academic freedom and feels that conflict in the classroom is a positive learning tool. He feels these students will work through this disagreement on their own. He says the SOC-R is too radical and has fueled the debate instead of contributing to it.

The dean has asked you, the department chair, to "take care of the matter," and you do not know where to begin. You had not signed up to deal with this type of issue when you agreed to become department chair, and now you wonder whether this is something that should be handled elsewhere. You agree it is an academic issue, yet you feel lost as to where to begin.

Considerations in Addressing This Issue

Like many situations in higher education, this case study illustrates a situation where all individuals involved feel as though they are being fair and doing the best they can. We offer the following questions as a method to explore your own paradigm and to reflect on how you can begin to look at these issues from a different perspective.

- What do you perceive to be the issues? Ask a colleague of color to read the case study and identify the issues; see whether they are the same issues you would perceive. Why might they be different?
- What are the identity development issues impacting white students?

- What are the identity development issues impacting students of color?
- To be effective as a faculty member in any discipline, what multicultural awareness, knowledge, and skills do you need?
- How can you be sure that the faculty member teaching the class has the knowledge and skills required to handle these types of conversations?
- How would you work with the faculty member to improve the relationship with white students and students of color?
- What multicultural skills is the dean lacking in this situation, and how would you work with the dean to enhance the levels of awareness?
- How would you approach the students of color in this situation?
- How would you approach the white students in this situation?
- What practices would you employ to get them to listen, dialogue, and empathize with students of color?
- What are the identity development issues impacting the faculty member, and how can the instructor be more empathetic to the concerns of white students?
- What are the identity development issues impacting the dean, and how can that person be more involved in the situation so that some understanding of and comfort with diversity issues occur?
- How would you characterize the campus culture based on what the students say about this classroom dialogue? Should this culture be changed?
- What campus resources are available to you for assistance in this situation?

Conclusions

We began this monograph by stating that it is our goal to challenge, inspire, and promote dialogue about these issues. The case exemplifies the complex and often convoluted nature of dealing with individuals, perceptions of the environment, the culture, and the impact of campus issues. Depending on a person's worldview, this case study will be interpreted differently, which is why we are not providing a recipe for the solution of this case. Each campus will have a different solution that depends on the perceptions of those involved. Yet because racial and ethnic representation continues to be low in higher education, educators often forget to consider the worldview of the minority—a view that is often very different from that of the dominant white culture. Case studies are a good tool to promote learning and understanding. The more discussion this case can prompt, the more likely learning will take place.

If readers of this case study see a clear and easy answer, then they do not understand the issues. And if they do not understand the issues, much more is needed to bring this person around; the question then becomes, Who will be responsible to educate this individual?

References

Abalos, D. T. (1986). *Latinos in the United States: The sacred and the political.* Notre Dame, IN: University of Notre Dame Press.

Acuña, R. (1988). *Occupied America: A history of Chicanos* (3rd ed.). New York: HarperCollins.

Adams, M. (2001). Core processes of racial identity development. In C. L. Wijeyesinghe and B. W. Jackson III (Eds.), *New perspectives on racial identity development: A theoretical and practical anthology* (pp. 209–242). New York: New York University Press.

Anderson, J. D. (2002). Race in American higher education: Historical perspectives on current conditions. In W. A. Smith, P. G. Altbach, and K. Lomotey (Eds.), *The racial crisis in American higher education: Continuing challenges for the twenty-first century* (pp. 3–22). Albany: State University of New York Press.

Arnett, J. J. (2000). Emerging adulthood: A theory of development from the late teens through the twenties. *American Psychologist, 55*(5), 469–480.

Asante, M. K. (1987). *The Afrocentric idea.* Philadelphia: Temple University Press.

Asante, M. K. (1991). *Afrocentricity.* Trenton, NJ: Africa World Press.

Atkinson, D. R., and Hackett, G. (1998). *Counseling diverse populations* (2nd ed.). Boston: McGraw-Hill.

Atkinson, D. R., Morten, G., and Sue, D. W. (1979). *Counseling American minorities* (1st ed.). Dubuque, IA: William C. Brown.

Atkinson, D. R., Morten, G., and Sue, D. W. (1989). *Counseling American minorities* (3rd ed.). Dubuque, IA: William C. Brown.

Atkinson, D. R., Morten, G., and Sue, D. W. (1998). *Counseling American minorities: A cross cultural perspective* (5th ed.). San Francisco: McGraw-Hill.

Baldwin, J. A., Duncan, J. A., and Bell, Y. R. (1992). Assessment of African self consciousness among Black students from two college environments. In A.K.H. Burlew, W. C. Banks, H. P. McAdoo, and D. A. Azibo (Eds.), *African American psychology: Theory, research, and practice* (pp. 283–299). Newbury Park, CA: Sage.

Banks, J. A. (1981). The stages of ethnicity: Implications for curriculum reform. In J. A. Banks (Ed.), *Multi-ethnic education: Theory and practice* (pp. 129–139). Boston: Allyn & Bacon.

Banks, M. (1996). *Ethnicity: Anthropological constructions*. London: Routledge.

Baxter Magolda, M. B. (2000). Teaching to promote holistic learning and development. In M. B. Baxter Magolda (Ed.), *Teaching to promote intellectual and personal maturity: Incorporating students' worldviews and identities into the learning process*. New Directions for Teaching and Learning, no. 82 (pp. 88–99). San Francisco: Jossey-Bass.

Bell, L. A. (1997). Theoretical foundations for social justice education. In M. Adams, L. A. Bell, and P. Griffin (Eds.), *Teaching for diversity and social justice: A sourcebook* (pp. 3–15). New York: Routledge.

Berzon, B. (1988). Permanent partners: Building gay and lesbian relationships that last. New York: E. P. Dutton.

Birman, D. (1994). Acculturation and human diversity in a multicultural society. In E. J. Trickett, R. J. Watts, and D. Birman (Eds.), *Human diversity: Perspectives on people in context* (pp. 261–284). San Francisco: Jossey-Bass.

Bowman, P. J., and Smith, W. A. (2002). Racial ideology in the campus community: Emerging cross-ethnic differences and challenges. In W. A. Smith, P. G. Altbach, and K. Lomotey (Eds.), *The racial crisis in American higher education: Continuing challenges for the twenty-first century* (pp. 103–120). Albany: State University of New York Press.

Brookfield, S. D. (1995). *Becoming a critically reflective teacher*. San Francisco: Jossey-Bass.

Callahan, P. M. (1994). Equity in higher education: The state role. In M. J. Justiz, R. Wilson, and L. G. Bjork (Eds.), *Minorities in higher education*. Phoenix: American Council on Education/Oryx.

Carney, C. G., and Kahn, K. B. (1984). Building competencies for effective cross-cultural counseling. A developmental view. *The Counseling Psychologist, 12*(1), 111–119.

Cass, V. (1979). Homosexual identity formation: A theoretical model. *Journal of Homosexuality, 4,* 219–235.

Cass, V. (1984). Homosexual identity formation: Testing a theoretical model. *Journal of Sex Research, 20,* 143–167.

Chan, C. S. (1989). Issues of identity development among Asian-American lesbians and gay men. *Journal of Counseling and Development, 68*(1), 16–20.

Chestang, L. W. (1984). Racial and personal identity in the black experience. In B. White (Ed.), *Color in a white society* (pp. 83–94). Silver Springs, MD: NASW.

Chickering, A. W., and Reisser, L. (1993). *Education and identity* (2nd ed.). San Francisco: Jossey-Bass.

Choney, S. K., Berryhill-Paapke, E., and Robbins, R. R. (1995). The acculturation of American Indians: Developing frameworks for research and practice. In J. G. Ponterotto, J. M. Casas, L. A. Suzuki, and C. M. Alexander (Eds.), *Handbook of multicultural counseling* (pp. 73–92). Thousand Oaks, CA: Sage.

Collins, P. H. (1990). *Black feminist thought: Knowledge, consciousness, and politics of empowerment*. Boston: Unwin Hyman.

Corey, G. (2001). *Theory and practice of counseling and psychology*. Belmont, CA: Brooks Cole.

Cross, W. E., Jr. (1971). The Negro-to-black conversion experience. *Black World, 20,* 13–27.

Cross, W. E., Jr. (1987). A two-factor theory of black identity: Implications for the study of identity development in minority children. In J. S. Phinney and M. J. Rotherham (Eds.), *Children's ethnic socialization: Pluralism and development* (pp. 117–133). Newbury Park, CA: Sage.

Cross, W. E., Jr. (1991). *Shades of black.* Philadelphia: Temple University Press.

Cross, W. E., Jr. (1995). The psychology of nigrescence: Revising the Cross model. In J. G. Ponterotto, J. M. Casas, L. A. Suzuki, and C. M. Alexander (Eds.), *Handbook of multicultural counseling* (pp. 93–122). Thousand Oaks, CA: Sage.

Cross, W. E., Jr., and Vandiver, B. J. (2001) Nigrescence theory and measurement: Introducing the Cross racial identity scale (CRIS). In J. G. Ponterotto, J. M. Casas, L. M. Suzuki, and C. M. Alexander (Eds.), *Handbook of multicultural counseling* (2nd ed.), pp. 371–393. Thousand Oaks, CA: Sage.

D'Augelli, A. R. (1994). Identity development and sexual orientation: Toward a model of lesbian, gay, and bisexual development. In E. J. Trickett, R. J. Watts, and D. Birman (Eds.), *Human diversity: Perspectives on people in context* (pp. 312–333). San Francisco: Jossey-Bass.

D'Augelli, A. R., and Hershberger, S. L. (1993). African American undergraduates on a predominantly white campus: Academic factors, social networks, and campus climate. *Journal of Negro Education, 62,* 67–81.

Deaux, K. (1993). *Social psychology in the 90s* (6th ed.). Pacific Grove, CA: Brooks/Cole.

Erikson, E. (1968). *Identity: Youth and crisis.* New York: Norton.

Erikson, E. H. (1964). *Insight and responsibility.* New York: Norton.

Espin, O. M. (1987a). Issues of identity in the psychology of Latina lesbians. In Boston Lesbian Psychology Collective (Eds.), *Lesbian psychologies* (pp. 35–51). Urbana: University of Illinois Press.

Espin, O. M. (1987b). Psychotherapy with Hispanic women: Some considerations. In P. Pedersen (Ed.), *Handbook of cross-cultural counseling and therapy* (pp. 165–171). Westport, CT: Greenwood.

Espiritu, Y. L. (1994). The intersection of race, ethnicity, and class: The multiple identities of second-generation Filipinos. *Identities, 1*(2–3), 249–273.

Evans, N. J., Forney, D. S., and Guido-DiBrito, F. (1998). *Student development in college: Theory, research, and practice.* San Francisco: Jossey-Bass.

Fassinger, R. E., and Miller, B. A. (1996). Validation of an inclusive model of sexual minority identity formation on a sample of gay men. *Journal of Homosexuality, 32*(2), 53–78.

Feagin, J. R. (2000). *Racist America: Roots, current realities, and future reparations.* New York: Routledge.

Feagin, J. R., Vera, H., and Imani, N. (1996). *The agony of education: Black students at white colleges and universities.* New York: Routledge.

Feliz-Ortiz de la Garza, M., Newcomb, M. D., and Myers, H. F. (1995). A multidimensional measure of cultural identity for Latino and Latina adolescents. In A. M. Padilla (Ed.), *Hispanic psychology: Critical issues in theory and research* (pp. 30–42). Thousand Oaks, CA: Sage.

Ferdman, B. M., and Gallegos, P. I. (2001). Racial identity development and Latinos in the United States. In C. L. Wijeyesinghe and B. W. Jackson III (Eds.), *New perspectives on racial identity development: A theoretical and practical anthology* (pp. 32–66). New York: New York University Press.

Foster, M., and Perry, L. R. (1982). Self evaluation among blacks. *Social Work, 27*(1), 60–66.

Frable, D.E.S. (1993). Being and feeling unique: Statistical deviance and psychological marginality. *Journal of Personality, 61*(1), 85–111.

Freire, P. (1987). *Pedagogy of the oppressed.* New York: Continuum.

Fries-Britt, S. (2000). Identity development of high ability black collegians. In M. B. Baxter Magolda (Ed.), *Teaching to promote intellectual and personal maturity: Incorporating students' worldviews and identities into the learning process* (pp. 55–66). New Directions for Teaching and Learning, no. 82. San Francisco: Jossey-Bass.

Garcia, M., and Smith, D. G. (1996). Reflecting inclusiveness in the college curriculum. In L. I. Rendon and R. O. Hope (Eds.), *Educating a new majority: Transforming America's educational system for diversity* (pp. 265–288). San Francisco: Jossey-Bass.

Garza, R. T., and Gallegos, P. I. (1995). Environmental influences and personal choice: A humanistic perspective on acculturation. In A. M. Padilla (Ed.), *Hispanic psychology: Critical issues in theory and research* (pp. 3–14). Thousand Oaks, CA: Sage.

Gay, G. (1984). Implications of selected models of ethnic identity development for educators. *Journal of Negro Education, 54*(1), 43–52.

Gloria, A. M., and Pope-Davis, D. B. (1997). Cultural ambiance: The importance of a culturally aware learning environment in the training and education of counselors. In D. B. Pope-Davis and H.L.K. Coleman (Eds.), *Multicultural counseling competencies: Assessment, education, training, and supervision* (pp. 242–259). Thousand Oaks, CA: Sage.

Gloria, A. M., Robinson Kurpius, S. E., Hamilton, K. D., and Willson, M. S. (1999). African American students' persistence at a predominantly white university: Influences of social support, university comfort, and self-beliefs. *Journal of College Student Development, 40,* 257–268.

Goodman, D. J. (2001). *Promoting diversity and social justice: Educating people from privileged groups.* Thousand Oaks, CA: Sage.

Hardiman, R. (2001). Reflections on white identity development theory. In C. L. Wijeyesinghe and B. W. Jackson (Eds.), *New perspectives on racial identity development: A theoretical and practical anthology* (pp. 108–128). New York: New York University.

Hardiman, R., and Jackson, B. W. (1997). Conceptual foundation for social justice courses. In M. Adams, L. A. Bell, and P. Griffin (Eds.), *Teaching for diversity and social justice: A sourcebook* (pp. 16–29). New York: Routledge.

Harvey, W. B. (2001). *Minorities in higher education, 2000–2001: Eighteenth annual status report.* Washington, DC: American Council on Education.

Helms, J. E. (1990). *"Womanist" identity attitudes: An alternative to feminism in counseling theory and research.* College Park: University of Maryland.

Helms, J. E. (1992). *Black and white racial identity: Theory, research, and practice.* New York: Praeger.

Helms, J. E. (1994). The conceptualization of racial identity and other racial constructs. In E. J. Trickett, R. J. Watts, and D. Birman (Eds.), *Human diversity: Perspectives on people in context* (pp. 285–311). San Francisco: Jossey-Bass.

Helms, J. E. (2000). *A race is a nice thing to have: A guide to being a white person or understanding the white persons in your life.* Topeka, KS: Content Communications.

Helms, J. E., and Cook, D. A. (1999). *Using race and culture in counseling in psychotherapy: Theory and process.* Needham Heights, MA: Allyn & Bacon.

Helms, J. E., and Piper, R. E. (1994). Implications of racial identity theory for vocational psychology. *Journal of Vocational Psychology, 44,* 124–128.

Ho, M. K. (1987). *Family therapy with ethnic minorities.* Newbury Park, CA: Sage.

Hoare, H. C. (1994). Psychosocial identity development in United States society: Its role in fostering exclusion of cultural others. In E. P. Salett and D. R. Koslow (Eds.), *Race, ethnicity, and self: Identity in multicultural perspective* (pp. 24–41). Washington, DC: National Multicultural Institute.

Hobgood, M. E. (2000). *Dismantling privilege: An ethics of accountability.* Cleveland: Pilgrim Press.

hooks, b. (1994). *Teaching to transgress: Education as the practice of freedom.* New York: Routledge.

Horse, P. G. (2001). Reflections on American Indian identity. In C. L. Wijeyesinghe and B. W. Jackson III (Eds.), *New perspectives on racial identity development: A theoretical and practical anthology* (pp. 91–107). New York: New York University Press.

Howard-Hamilton, M. F. (2000). Creating a culturally responsive learning environment for African American students. In M. B. Baxter Magolda (Ed.), *Teaching to promote intellectual and personal maturity: Incorporating students' worldviews and identities into the learning process* (pp. 45–53). New Directions for Teaching and Learning, no. 82. San Francisco: Jossey-Bass.

Howard-Hamilton, M. F., and Hinton, K. G. (2002). *Multicultural competence: Research developments, implications, and challenges.* Paper presented at the Roger Winston Student Development Institute, July, Athens, GA.

Huang, L. N. (1994). An integrative approach to clinical assessment and intervention with Asian American adolescents. *Journal of Clinical Child Psychology, 23,* 21–31.

Hurtado, S. (1996). The campus racial climate: Context of conflict. In C.S.V. Turner, M. Garcia, A. Nora, and L. I. Rendon (Eds.), *Racial and ethnic diversity in higher education* (pp. 485–506). Boston: Pearson Custom Publishing.

Hurtado, S., Milem, J., Clayton-Pedersen, A., and Allen, W. (1999). *Enacting diverse learning environments: Improving the climate for racial/ethnic diversity in higher education.* ASHE-ERIC Higher Education Report, vol. 26, no. 8. Washington, DC: Graduate School of Education and Human Development, The George Washington University.

Ibrahim, F., Ohnishi, H., and Sandhu, D. S. (1997). Asian American identity development: A culture specific model for South Asian Americans. *Journal of Multicultural Counseling and Development, 25,* 34–50.

Icard, L. (1985–86). Black gay men and conflicting social identities: Sexual orientation versus racial identity. *Journal of Social Work, 4*(1–2), 83–93.

Ivey, A., Ivey, M., and Simek-Morgan, L. (Eds.). (1993). *Counseling and psychotherapy: A multicultural perspective.* Boston: Allyn & Bacon.

Jackson, B. W. (1976). Black identity development. In L. H. Golubchick and B. Persky (Eds.), *Urban social and educational issues* (pp. 158–164). Dubuque, IA: Kendall Hunt.

Jackson, B. W. (2001). Black identity development: Further analysis and elaboration. In C. L. Wijeyesinghe and B. W. Jackson (Eds.), *New perspectives on racial identity development: A theoretical and practical anthology* (pp. 8–31). New York: New York University Press.

Johnson, S. D. (1997). The multiple hats of identity: Addressing the various components of African American identity in student development. *College Student Affairs Journal, 16*(2), 65–72.

Jones, S. R. (1997). Voices of identity and difference: A qualitative exploration of the multiple dimensions of identity development in women college students. *Journal of College Student Development, 38*(4), 376–386.

Jones, S. R., and McEwen, M. K. (2000). A conceptual model of multiple dimensions of identity. *Journal of College Student Development, 41*(4), 405–415.

Jones, T., and Young, G. A. (1997). Classroom dynamics: Disclosing the hidden curriculum. In A. I. Morey and M. K. Kitano (Eds.), *Multicultural course transformation in higher education: A broader truth* (pp. 89–102). Boston: Allyn & Bacon.

Josselson, R. (1987). *Finding herself: Pathways to identity development in women.* San Francisco. Jossey-Bass.

Josselson, R. (1992). *The space between us: Exploring the dimensions of human relationships.* San Francisco: Jossey-Bass.

Karenga, M. (1980). *Kawaida theory.* Los Angeles: Kawaida Publications.

Keefe, S. E., and Padilla, A. M. (1987). *Chicano ethnicity.* Albuquerque: University of New Mexico Press.

Kerwin, C., and Ponterotto, J. G. (1995). Biracial identity development: Theory and research. In J. Ponterotto, J. M. Casas, L. A. Suzuki, and C. M. Alexander (Eds.), *Handbook of multicultural counseling* (pp. 199–217). Newbury Park, CA: Sage.

Kim, J. (1981). Processes of Asian American identity development: A study of Japanese American women's perceptions of their struggle to achieve positive identities as Americans of Asian ancestry. Unpublished doctoral dissertation, University of Massachusetts, Amherst.

Kim, J. (2001). Asian American identity development theory. In C. L. Wijeyesinghe and B. W. Jackson III (Eds.), *New perspectives on racial identity development: A theoretical and practical anthology* (pp. 67–90). New York: New York University Press.

King, P. M. (2000). Learning to make reflective judgments. In M. B. Baxter Magolda (Ed.), *Teaching to promote intellectual and personal maturity: Incorporating students' worldviews and identities into the learning process* (pp. 15–26). New Directions for Teaching and Learning, no. 82. San Francisco: Jossey-Bass.

Knight, G. P., Bernal, M. E., Garza, C. A., and Cota, M. K. (1993). A social cognitive model of the development of ethnic idenity and ethnically-based behaviors. In M. E. Bernal and G. P. Knight (Eds.), *Ethnic identity formation and transmission among Hispanics and other minorities* (pp. 213–234). Albany: State University of New York Press.

LaCounte, D. W. (1987). American Indian students in college. In D. J. Wright (Ed.), *Responding to the needs of today's minority students* (pp. 65–79). New Directions for Student Services, no. 38. San Francisco: Jossey-Bass.

LaFromboise, T. D., Heyle, A. M., and Ozer, E. J. (1990). Changing and diverse roles of women in American Indian cultures. *Sex Roles, 22*(7/8), 455–476.

LaFromboise, T. D., and Rowe, W. (1983). Skills training for bicultural competence: Rationale and application. *Journal of Counseling Psychology, 30*(4), 589–595.

LaFromboise, T. D., Trimble, J. E., and Mohatt, G. V. (1990). Counseling intervention and American Indian tradition: An integrative approach. *The Counseling Psychologist, 18*(4), 628–654.

Lang, M., and Ford, C. A. (Eds.). (1992). *Strategies for retaining minority students in higher education.* Springfield, IL: Charles Thomas.

Loiacano, D. K. (1989). Gay identity issues among black Americans: Racism, homophobia, and the need for validation. *Journal of Counseling and Development, 68*(1), 21–25.

Lomawaima, K. T. (2000). Tribal sovereigns: Reframing research in American Indian education. *Harvard Educational Review, 70*(1), 1–21.

Lowell, B. L., and Suro, R. (2002). *The improving educational profile of Latino immigrants.* Washington, DC: Pew Hispanic Center. [http://www.pewhispanic.org]

Maekawa Kodama, C., McEwen, M. K., Liang, C.T.H., and Lee, S. (2002). An Asian American perspective on psychosocial development theory. In M. K. McEwen and others (Eds.), *Working with Asian American college students* (pp. 45–59). New Directions for Student Services, no. 97. San Francisco: Jossey-Bass.

Marcia, J. E. (1966). Development and validation of ego status. *Journal of Personality and Social Psychology, 3,* 551–558.

Marcia, J. E. (1980). Identity in adolescence. In J. Adelson (Ed.), *Handbook of adolescent psychology* (pp. 159–187). New York: Wiley.

McCarn, S. R., and Fassinger, R. E. (1996). Revisioning sexual minority identity formation: A new model of lesbian identity and its implications for counseling and research. *Counseling Psychologist, 24*(3), 508–524.

McEwen, M. K. (1996). New perspectives on identity development. In S. R. Komives and D. B. Woodward, Jr. (Eds.), *Student services: A handbook for the profession* (3rd ed., pp. 188–217). San Francisco: Jossey-Bass.

McEwen, M. K., Roper, L. D., Bryant, D. R., and Langa, M. J. (1990). Incorporating the development of African American students into psychosocial theories of student development. *Journal of College Student Development, 31*(5), 429–436.

McIntosh, P. (1988). *White privilege and male privilege: A personal account of coming to see correspondence through work in women's studies.* Working paper 189. Wellesley, MA: Center for Research on Women.

McIntosh, P. (1998). White privilege, color, and crime: A personal account. In C. R. Mann, and M. S. Zatz (Eds.), *Images of color and images of crime: Readings* (pp. 207–216). Los Angeles: Roxbury.

McNamera, K., and Rickard, K. M. (1998). Feminist identity development: Implications for feminist therapy with women. In D. R. Atkinson and G. Hackett (Eds.), *Counseling diverse populations* (2nd ed., pp. 271–282). Boston: McGraw-Hill.

Miller, D. T., and Prentice, D. A. (1999). Some consequences of a belief in group essence: The category divide hypothesis. In D. A. Prentice and D. T. Miller (Eds.), *Cultural divides: Understanding and overcoming group conflict* (pp. 213–238). New York: Russell Sage Foundation.

Mohr, J., and Fassinger, R. (2000). Measuring dimensions of lesbian and gay male experience. *Measurement and Evaluation in Counseling and Development, 33*(2), 66–90.

Myers, L. J. (1988). *Understanding an Afrocentric world view: Introduction to an optimal psychology.* Dubuque, IA: Kendall/Hunt.

Myers, L. J., and Speight, S. L. (1994). Optimal theory and the psychology of human diversity. In E. J. Trickett, R. J. Watts, and D. Bitman (Eds.), *Human diversity: Perspectives on people in context* (pp. 101–114). San Francisco: Jossey-Bass.

Myers, L. J., and others. (1991). Identity development and worldview: Toward an optimal conceptualization. *Journal of Counseling and Development, 70,* 54–63.

Nicassio, P. (1985). The psychosocial adjustment of the Southeast Asian refugee: An overview of empirical findings and theoretical models. *Journal of Cross-Cultural Psychology, 16*(2), 153–173.

Ortiz, A. M. (2000). Expressing cultural identity in the learning community: Opportunities and challenges. In M. B. Baxter Magolda (Ed.), *Teaching to promote intellectual and personal maturity: Incorporating students' worldviews and identities into the learning process* (pp. 67–80). New Directions for Teaching and Learning, no. 82. San Francisco: Jossey-Bass.

Ortiz, A., and Rhoads, R. A. (2000). Deconstructing whiteness as part of a multicultural educational framework: From theory to practice. *Journal of College Student Development, 41*(1), 81–93.

Ossana, S. M., Helms, J. E., and Leonard, M. M. (1992). Do "womanist" identity attitudes influence college women's self-esteem and perceptions of environmental bias? *Journal of Counseling and Development, 70*(1), 402–408.

Pascarella, E. T., and Terenzini, P. T. (1991). *How college affects students.* San Francisco: Jossey-Bass.

Perka, P. L., Matherly, C. A., Fishman, D. E., and Ridge, R. H. (1992). Using photographs to examine environmental perceptions of African American and white Greek members: A qualitative study. *College Student Affairs Journal, 12*(1), 7–16.

Peterson, S. (2000). Multicultural perspective on middle-class women's identity development. *Journal of Counseling and Development, 78*(1), 63–71.

Phinney, J. S. (1990). Ethnic identity in adolescents and adults: Review of the research. *Psychological Bulletin, 108,* 499–514.

Phinney, J. S. (1992). The multigroup ethnic identity measure: A new scale for use with diverse groups. *Journal of Adolescent Research, 7,* 156–176.

Phinney, J. S. (1996). Understanding ethnic diversity. *American Behavioral Scientist, 40*(2), 143–153.

Phinney, J. S., and Alipuria, L. L. (1990). Ethnic identity in college students from four ethnic groups. *Journal of Adolescences, 13,* 171–183.

Phinney, J. S., and Chavira, V. (1992). Ethnic identity and self-esteem: An exploratory longitudinal study. *Journal of Adolescence, 15,* 271–281.

Ponterotto, J. G., Casas, J. M., Suzuki, L. A., and Alexander, C. M. (2001). *Handbook of multicultural counseling.* Thousand Oaks, CA: Sage.

Ponterotto, J. G., and Pedersen, P. B. (1993). *Preventing prejudice: A guide for counselors and educators.* Newbury Park, CA: Sage.

Pope, R. L. (1998). The relationship between psychosocial development and racial identity of black college students. *Journal of Counseling and Development, 39*(1), 273–282.

Poston, W.S.C. (1990). The biracial identity development model: A needed addition. *Journal of Counseling and Development, 69,* 152–155.

Raetz, T., and Lease, J. (2002). *The construction of identity.* Unpublished manuscript. Athens: University of Georgia.

Reynolds, A. L., and Pope, R. L. (1991). The complexities of diversity: Exploring multiple oppressions. *Journal of Counseling and Development, 70*(1), 174–180.

Reisser, L. (1995). Revisiting the seven vectors. *Journal of College Student Development, 36*(6), 505–511.

Robinson, T. L. (1993). The intersections of gender, class, race, and culture: On seeing clients whole. *Journal of Multicultural Counseling and Development, 21*(1), 50–59.

Robinson, T. L., and Howard-Hamilton, M. F. (1994). An Afrocentric paradigm: Foundation for a healthy self-image and healthy interpersonal relationships. *Journal of Mental Health Counseling, 16*(3), 327–340.

Robinson, T. L., and Howard-Hamilton, M. F. (2000). *The convergence of race, ethnicity, and gender: Multiple identities in counseling.* Upper Saddle River, NJ: Merrill–Prentice Hall.

Robinson, T. L., and Ward, J. V. (1991). A belief in self far greater than anyone's disbelief: Cultivating resistance among African American adolescents. *Women and Therapy, 11,* 87–103.

Root, M. P. (1990). Resolving "other" status: Identity of biracial individuals. *Women and Therapy, 9*(1–2), 185–205.

Rowe, W., Bennett, S. K., and Atkinson, D. R (1994). White racial identity models: A critique and alternate proposal. *The Counseling Psychologist, 22,* 129–146.

Saddlemire, J. R. (1996). Qualitative study of white second-semester undergraduates' attitudes toward African American undergraduates at a predominantly white institution. *Journal of College Student Development, 37,* 684–691.

Sanford, N. (1962). *The American college.* New York: Wiley.

Schmidt, P. (2003, January 24). Bush asks Supreme Court to strike down U. of Michigan's affirmative-action policy. *Chronicle of Higher Education,* A20–A21.

Scheurich, J. J., and Young, M. D. (2002). White racism among white faculty: From critical understanding to antiracist activism. In W. A. Smith, P. G. Altbach, and K. Lomotey (Eds.), *The racial crisis in American higher education: Continuing challenges for the twenty-first century* (pp. 221–242). Albany: State University of New York Press.

Sedlacek, W. E. (1999). Black students on white campuses: Twenty years of research. *Journal of College Student Development, 40,* 538–550.

Selingo, J. (2003, January 31). The broad reach of the Michigan cases: The Supreme Court will examine public-university admissions, but private colleges will be affected too. *Chronicle of Higher Education,* A21–A22.

Smith, D. (1996). Organizing for diversity: Fundamental issues. In C. Turner, M. Garcia, A. Nora, and L. I. Rendon (Eds.), *Racial and Ethnic Diversity in Higher Education* (pp. 532–541). Boston: Person Custom Publishing.

Spring, J. (1994). *Wheels in the head: Educational philosophies of authority, freedom, and culture from Socrates to Paulo Freire.* Boston: McGraw-Hill.

Spring, J. (1999). *Wheels in the head: Educational philosophies of authority, freedom, and culture from Socrates to human rights* (2nd ed.). Boston: McGraw-Hill.

Spring, J. (2001). *Deculturalization and the struggle for equality: A brief history of the education of dominated cultures in the United States.* Boston: McGraw-Hill.

Steele, C. M., and Aronson, J. (1995). Stereotype threat and the intellectual test performance of African Americans. *Journal of Personality and Social Psychology, 69*(5), 797–811.

Strange, C., and Banning, J. (2001). *Educating by design: Creating campus learning environments that work.* San Francisco: Jossey-Bass.

Sue, D. W. (1989). Racial/cultural identity development among Asian Americans: Counseling/therapy implications. *Journal of the Asian American Psychological Association, 13,* 80–86.

Sue, D. W., and Sue, D. (1990). *Counseling the culturally different: Theory and practice.* New York: Wiley.

Sue, D. W., and Sue, D. (1999). *Counseling the culturally different: Theory and practice* (3rd ed.). New York: Wiley.

Sue, D. W., and Sue, D. (2003). *Counseling the culturally diverse: Theory and practice* (4th ed.). New York: Wiley.

Szapocznik, J., and Kurtines, W. (1980). Acculturation, biculturalism, and adjustment among Cuban Americans. In A. M. Padilla (Ed.), *Acculturation theories, models, and some new findings* (pp. 139–159). Boulder, CO: Westview Press.

Takaki, R. (1993). *A different mirror: A history of multicultural America.* Boston: Little, Brown.

Tatum, B. D. (1992). Talking about race, learning about racism: The application of racial identity development theory in the classroom. *Harvard Educational Review, 62*(1), 1–23.

Tatum, B. D. (1996). Talking about race, learning about racism: The application of racial identity development and theory in the classroom. In C.S.V. Turner, M. Garcia, A. Nora, and L. I. Rendon (Eds.), *Racial and ethnic diversity in higher education* (pp. 150–169). Needham Heights, MA: Simon & Schuster.

Tatum, B. D. (1997). *Why are all the black kids sitting together in the cafeteria? And other conversations about race.* New York: Basic Books.

Taub, D. J., and McEwen, M. K. (1992). The relationship of racial identity attitudes to autonomy and mature interpersonal relationships in black and white undergraduate women. *Journal of College Student Development, 33*(5), 439–446.

Taylor, C. M., and Howard-Hamilton, M. F. (1995). Student involvement and racial identity attitudes among African American males. *Journal of College Student Development, 36,* 330–336.

Terry, R. W. (1977). *For whites only.* Grand Rapids, MI: William B. Erdmans.

Thompson, C. E., and Carter, R. T. (1997). An overview and elaboration of Helms' racial identity development theory. In C. E. Thompson and R. T. Carter (Eds.), *Racial identity theory: Applications to individual, group, and organizational interventions* (pp. 15–32). Mahwah, NJ: Erlbaum.

Torres, V. (1999). Validation of a bicultural orientation model for Hispanic college students. *Journal of College Student Development, 40*(3), 285–299.

Torres, V. (forthcoming). Influences on the ethnic identity development of Latino college students in the first two years of college. *Journal of College Student Development.*

Torres, V., and Phelps, R. E. (1997). Hispanic American acculturation and ethnic identity: A bicultural model. *College Student Affairs Journal, 17*(1), 53–68.

Torres, V., Winston, R. B., Jr., and Cooper, D. L. (2003). Hispanic American students' cultural orientation: Does geographic location, institutional type, or level of stress have an effect? *NASPA Journal, 40*(2). [http://publications.naspa.org/naspajournal/vol40/iss2/art10]

Troiden, R. R. (1989). The formation of homosexual identities. *Journal of Homosexuality, 17*(1–2), 43–74.

Uba, L. (1994). *Asian Americans: Personality patterns, identity, and mental health.* New York: Guilford Press.

Vandiver, B. J. (2001). Psychological nigrescence revisited: Introduction and overview. *Multicultural Counseling and Development, 29,* 165–173.

Wellman, D. (1977). *Portraits of white racism.* Cambridge, UK: Cambridge University Press.

Wijeyesinghe, C. L. (2001). Racial identity in multiracial people: An alternative paradigm. In C. L. Wijeyesinghe and B. W. Jackson III (Eds.), *New perspectives on racial identity development: A theoretical and practical anthology* (pp. 129–152). New York: New York University Press.

Winston, R. B., Jr., Miller, T. K., and Cooper, D. L. (1999). *Preliminary technical manual for the student developmental task and lifestyle assessment.* Athens, GA: Student Development Associates.

Wlodkowski, R. J., and Ginsberg, M. B. (1995). *Diversity and motivation: Culturally responsive teaching.* San Francisco: Jossey-Bass.

Yeh, C. J., and Huang, K. (1996). The collectivistic nature of ethnic identity development among Asian-American college students. *Adolescence, 31*(Fall), 645–661.

Yinger, J. M. (1994). *Ethnicity: Source of strength? Source of conflict?* Albany: State University of New York Press.

Yoshioka, R. B., Tashima, N., Chew, M., and Maruse, K. (1981). *Mental health services for Pacific/Asian Americans.* San Francisco: Pacific Asian Mental Health Project.

Name Index

A

Abalos, D. T., 58
Acuña, R., 54
Adams, M., 18, 37
Alexander, C. M., 37
Alipuria, L. L., 37
Allen, W., 81
Anderson, J. D., 39
Arnett, J. J., 14–15
Aronson, J., 5
Asante, M. K., 47
Atkinson, D. R., 29, 34, 34–36, 61, 73

B

Baldwin, J. A., 46
Banks, J. A., 46
Banks, M., 4
Banning, J., 80, 81
Baxter Magolda, M. B., 96
Bell, L. A., 18, 19, 20
Bell, Y. R., 46
Bennett, S. K., 29
Bernal, M. E., 52
Berryhill-Paapke, E., 51
Berzon, B., 74
Birman, D., 5, 17
Bowman, P. J., 79, 93
Brookfield, S. D., 96
Bryant, D. R., 15, 16

C

Callahan, P. M., 82
Carney, C. G., 29
Carter, R. T., 41
Casas, J. M., 37
Cass, V., 73–74
Chan, C. S., 68, 69, 76
Chavira, V., 37
Chestang, L. W., 10
Chew, M., 62
Chickering, A. W., 3, 11, 13, 62
Choney, S. K., 51
Clayton-Pedersen, A., 81
Collins, P. H., 47–48
Cook, D. A., 27, 28, 29, 38
Cooper, D. L., 14, 58
Corey, G., 88
Cota, M. K., 52
Cross, W. E., Jr., 41, 4, 43, 44, 45, 68, 72, 76, 77

D

D'Augelli, A. R., 40, 76
Deaux, K., 68, 72–73
Duncan, J. A., 46

E

Erikson, E. H., 3, 9–11, 35
Espin, O. M., 69, 71
Espiritu, Y. L., 68
Evans, N. J., 14, 36, 76

F

Fassinger, R. E., 76
Feagin, J. R., 27, 40, 80, 93, 94, 95
Feliz-Ortiz de la Garza, M., 58

Ferdman, B. M., 54, 57
Fishman, D. E., 40
Ford, C. A., 40
Forney, D. S., 14, 36, 76
Foster, M., 10
Freire, P., 17, 19, 20, 86, 95, 98
Fries-Britt, S., 96

G

Gallegos, P. I., 7, 54, 57
Garcia, M., 98
Garza, C. A., 52
Garza, R. T., 7
Gay, G., 45
Ginsberg, M. B., 96
Gloria, A. M., 40
Goodman, D. J., 25, 26, 27, 28
Guido-DiBrito, F., 14, 36, 76

H

Hackett, G., 73
Hamilton, K. D., 40
Hardiman, R., 21, 22, 23, 24, 27,
    28, 29
Harvey, W. B., 4, 6
Helms, J. E., 3, 6, 7, 18, 27, 28, 29, 30,
    39, 76, 87
Hershberger, S. L., 40
Heyle, A. M., 49
Hinton, K. G., 87–88
Ho, M. K., 59
Hobgood, M. E., 27
hooks, b., 87, 96, 98
Horse, P. G., 49, 51–52
Howard-Hamilton, M. F., 35, 40, 47–48,
    69, 87–88, 96
Huang, K., 59
Huang, L. N., 59
Hurtado, S., 1, 2, 81

I

Ibrahim, F., 61
Icard, L., 69
Imani, N., 40, 80, 94

Ivey, A., 10
Ivey, M., 10

J

Jackson, B. W., 21, 22, 23, 24, 45–46
Johnson, S. D., 73
Jones, S. R., 68, 70, 71–72
Jones, T., 87
Josselson, R., 12–13, 76

K

Kahn, K. B., 29
Karenga, M., 47
Keefe, S. E., 53, 54–55
Kerwin, C., 64
Kim, J., 60–61
King, P. M., 96
Knight, G. P., 52
Kurtines, W., 58

L

LaCounte, D. W., 49
LaFromboise, T. D., 49
Lang, M., 40
Langa, M. J., 15, 16
Lease, J., 68
Lee, S., 62
Leonard, M. M., 77
Liang, C.T.H., 62
Loiacano, D. K., 68, 69, 76
Lomawaima, K. T., 49
Lowell, B. L., 59

M

Maekawa Kodaama, C., 62
Marcia, J. E., 11–12
Maruse, K., 62
Matherly, C. A., 40
McCarn, S. R., 76
McEwen, M. K., 15, 16, 62, 68,
    70, 80
McIntosh, P., 25, 27, 30–31, 95
McNamera, K., 77
Milem, J. A., 81
Miller, B. A., 76

Miller, D. T., 1, 2
Miller, T. K., 14
Mohatt, G. V., 5–0
Mohr, J., 76
Morten, G., 34, 61
Myers, H. F., 58
Myers, L. J., 37, 47

N
Newcomb, M. D., 58
Nicassio, P., 63

O
Ohnishi, H., 61
Ortiz, A. M., 28, 96
Ossana, S. M., 77
Ozer, E. J., 49

P
Padilla, A. M., 53, 54–55
Pascarella, E. T., 3, 40
Pedersen, P. B., 60
Perka, P. L., 40
Perry, L. R., 10
Peterson, S., 77
Phelps, R. E., 58
Phinney, J. S., 33, 36–37, 53
Piper, R. E., 27–28
Ponterotto, J. G., 37, 60, 64
Pope, R. L., 40, 68, 73
Pope-Davis, D. B., 40
Poston, W.S.C., 64–65
Prentice, D. A., 1, 2

R
Raetz, T., 68
Reisser, L., 3, 11, 13, 14, 62
Reynolds, A. L., 37, 68, 73
Rhoads, R. A., 27, 28, 29–30
Rickard, K. M., 77
Ridge, R. H., 40
Robbins, R. R., 51
Robinson Kurpius, S. E., 40
Robinson, T. L., 35, 47–48,
    68, 69

Root, M. P., 68, 73
Roper, L. D., 15, 16
Rowe, W., 29, 49

S
Saddlemire, J. R., 40
Sandhu, D. S., 61
Sanford, N., 11
Scheurich, J. J., 94
Schmidt, P., 2
Selingo, J., 2
Simek-Morgan, L., 10
Smith, D., 1, 81, 83, 93, 99
Smith, D. G., 98
Smith, W. A., 79
Speight, S. L., 37, 47
Spring, J., 18, 19, 20
Steele, C. M., 5
Strange, C., 80, 81
Sue, D., 33, 35, 69
Sue, D. W., 33, 34–36, 61, 69
Suro, R., 59
Suzuki, L. A., 37
Szapocznik, J., 58

T
Takaki, R., 18
Tashima, N., 62
Tatum, B. D., 2, 4, 5, 79, 87, 93, 94,
    96, 98
Taub, D. J., 15, 80
Taylor, C. M., 40
Terenzini, P. T., 3, 40
Terry, R. W., 29
Thompson, C. E., 41
Torres, V., 53, 55–57, 58
Trimble, J. E., 50
Troiden, R. R., 75

U
Uba, L., 61, 62–63

V
Vandiver, B. J., 42, 44
Vera, H., 40, 80, 94

W

Ward, J. V., 47
Wellman, D., 27
Wijeyesinghe, C. L., 64, 65
Willson, M. S., 40
Winston, R. B., Jr., 14, 58
Wlodkowski, R. J., 96

Y

Yeh, C. J., 59
Yinger, J. M., 6
Yoshioka, R. B., 62
Young, G. A., 87
Young, M. D., 94

Subject Index

A

Acculturation
  and biculturalism, 58
  and family/society domains, 62
  health model conceptualization of, 51
  linear models of, 53
  multidimensional models of, 53
  process, 7
  two-dimensional models of, 53
Administrators and campus diversity,
  82–86
African American identity development
  Afrocentricity framework in, 47
  college environment and, 39–41, 48
  feminist theory of, 47–48
  models and theories of, 39–48
  of multiple identities, 73
  nigrescence model of, 41–45
  psychosocial theories and, 15–16
  racism and, 39
  stage models of, 41–45
  in white institutions, 15
American Indian racial identity, 49–52
  acculturation and, 51
  and categories of Indianness, 50
  Indian values/consciousness in, 49–50,
    51–52
  theories, 49–52
  tribal sovereignty and, 49–50, 51–52
Asian American ethnic identity
  development
  and individualized differences, 62–64
  psychosocial model of, 62
  research and theory, 59–64
  salience of ethnicity in, 63–64
  social context in, 63–64
  stages of, 60–61

B

Banker's education, 20, 86
Biculturalism
  defined, 57–58
  models of, 58–59
Biracial identity development, 64–65
Black power movement, 41

C

Campus environment
  creating inclusiveness and diversity in,
    81–92
  dominant group culture in, 80–81
  expressions of cultural identity in, 84
  postmodern trends in, 79
  and racial identity development, 15,
    39–41
  structural diversity in, 81
Chicano ethnicity, loyalty and social
  orientation in, 54–55
Core identity, 70–72
Course content and diversity issues, 87
Cultural awareness and multiple
  identities, 71
Culture, defined, 6–7
Curriculum and inclusiveness in, 87–92, 94

D

Diversity, definition of, 4

E

Ego epigenesis, 10
Ego strengths, 10–11
Ethnic identity
    salience of, 63–64
    three-stage development model of,
        36–37
Ethnicity, definition of, 6

F

Factor model of multiracial identity
    (FMMI), 65
Faculty
    campus inclusiveness strategies for,
        86–99
    diversity, 98
Foreclosed identity, 11, 12

G

Gay and lesbian identity development,
    73–74
Gender identity formation
    of multiple identities, 71
    stages of, 76–77

I

Identity
    components of, 68
    defined, 9
    diffusion, 12, 13
    moratorium, 12, 36–37
Identity achievers, 12
Identity development theory
    foundational, 9–16
    implications for administrators,
        82–86
    implications for faculty, 86–99
Identity development
    cultural and societal impacts on,
        18–19
    environment's role in, 10, 15, 38
    identity crisis in, 11–12
    and social identity, 23–25

L

Latino identity development
    acculturation and, 55, 56
    biculturalism and, 57–58
    commonalities in, 53–54
    immigration and, 54
    Latino diversity and, 59
    models, 54–59

M

Minority identity development (MID)
    model, 34, 61
Multicultural competence
    behavioral patterns of, 88–92
    model, 34–35
Multicultural education framework, 29–30
Multiethnicity, 46
Multigroup ethnic identity measure
    (MEIM), 37
Multiple identity development, 67–78
    and core identity, 70–72
    contextual influences on, 70
    process, 70–73
    salient features of, 69
    and sexual orientation, 73–76
    of women, 76–78
Multiracial identity, 64–66
    factor model of, 65
    and oppression, 65

N

Native Americans. *See* American Indian
    identity development
Nuclear conflict, 10

O

Oppression
    deculturalization in, 20
    government-sanctioned, 49
    and multiracial identity choice, 65
    significant themes in, 20–21
    social, 21–26
    social identity development in, 23–25
    student development impacted by, 80
    and suppression of cultural identity, 54
    theories of, 18–23

Optimal theory applied to identity
    development (OTAID), 37–38

P
Personal identity
    in multiple identity development, 72
    in nigrescence theory, 41, 42
    tripartite development model of, 69
Privileged groups
    identity development of, 23–25
    impact of oppression and privilege on,
        25–27
Psychosocial development theories, 15–16,
    60–61, 62

R
Race
    defined, 6
    salience, 41, 42
    theories, 3–4
    and white socialization, 27–28
Racial choice of multiracial or biracial
    individuals, 64–66
Racial conflict
    and development of multiple identity, 71
    student opinions of, 1–2
Racial and ethnic identity development,
    17–31
    acculturation and, 52–53
    of Asian American students, 59–64
    of African American students, 15–16,
        39–48
    faculty's role in, 87
    of Latino students, 53–59
    multigroup models of, 33–38
    multiracial, 3, 64–66
    Native American, 49–52
    oppression and, 19–21, 23–25
    stereotyping and, 5–6
    and systematic racism and sexism, 18
    theoretical frameworks for, 33–66
    in traditional theories, 14–15
Racial stereotyping, 5–6, 18, 23, 56
Racial/cultural identity development
    (R/CID) model, 34–36

Racism
    and black racial identity development,
        39–40
    student dialogues and workshops on, 98
Reference group orientation, 41, 42

S
Sexual orientation identity formation
    and multiple identity issues, 76
    stages and processes in, 73–76
Social group, definition of, 7
Social identity theory, 23–25
    and multiple identity development, 72
Social oppression
    matrix, 21–23
    psychological and societal costs of,
        25–26
    psychosocial processes in, 22–23
Stereotype threat, 5
Student development theory
    developmental tasks (vectors) in,
        13–14
    and multiple identities, 3
    and stage theory, 11
Student journals, 87–92, 97

T
Teaching strategies for diversity, 94–97
Typology of Mexican American Ethnic
    Orientation, 55

W
"Wheels in the head" syndrome, 19
White identity development, 17
    interpersonal perspective on, 28–29
    racial identity in, 27–28, 30–31
    theories, 4, 5–6, 27–33
White dominant culture
    acculturation to, 52–53
    classroom/campus orientation to,
        92–94
    racism and oppression in, 18
Women's identity formation
    African American, 15–16, 47–48
    of multiple identities, 70–72, 76–78

About the ASHE-ERIC Higher Education Reports Series

Since 1983, the ASHE-ERIC Higher Education Report Series has been providing researchers, scholars, and practitioners with timely and substantive information on the critical issues facing higher education. Each monograph presents a definitive analysis of a higher education problem or issue, based on a thorough synthesis of significant literature and institutional experiences. Topics range from planning to diversity and multiculturalism, to performance indicators, to curricular innovations. The mission of the Series is to link the best of higher education research and practice to inform decision making and policy. The reports connect conventional wisdom with research and are designed to help busy individuals keep up with the higher education literature. Authors are scholars and practitioners in the academic community. Each report includes an executive summary, review of the pertinent literature, descriptions of effective educational practices, and a summary of key issues to keep in mind to improve educational policies and practice.

The Series is one of the most peer reviewed in higher education. A National Advisory Board made up of ASHE members reviews proposals. A National Review Board of ASHE scholars and practitioners reviews completed manuscripts. Six monographs are published each year and they are approximately 120 pages in length. The reports are widely disseminated through Jossey-Bass and John Wiley & Sons, and they are available online to subscribing institutions through Wiley InterScience (http://www.interscience.wiley.com).

Call for Proposals

The ASHE-ERIC Higher Education Report Series is actively looking for proposals. We encourage you to contact the editor, Dr. Adrianna Kezar, at kezar@usc.edu with your ideas. For detailed information about the Series, please visit http://www.eriche.org/publications/writing.html.

Advisory Board

Kenneth Feldman
SUNY at Stony Brook

Anna Ortiz
Michigan State University

James Fairweather
Michigan State University

Jerlando Jackson
University of Wisconsin

Melissa Anderson
University of Minnesota

Doug Toma
University of Pennsylvania

Amy Metcalfe
University of Arizona

Carol Colbeck
Pennsylvania State University

Consulting Editors
and Review Panelists

Deborah-Faye Carter
Indiana University
Judith Glazer-Raymo
Long Island University
Patrick Love
Kent State University
Anna Ortiz
Michigan State University

Robert Rhoads
Michigan State University
Marylu K. McEwen
University of Maryland
Raechele L. Pope
University at Buffalo

Recent Titles

Volume 29 ASHE-ERIC Higher Education Reports

1. Ensuring Quality and Productivity in Higher Education:
   An Analysis of Assessment Practices
   Susan M. Gates and Associates

2. Institutionalizing a Broader View of Scholarship Through Boyer's Four Domains
   John M. Braxton, William Luckey, and Patricia Helland

3. Transforming the Curriculum: Preparing Students for a Changing World
   Elizabeth A. Jones

4. Quality in Distance Education: Focus on On-Line Learning
   Katrina A. Meyer

5. Faculty Service Roles and the Scholarship of Engagement
   Kelly Ward

Volume 28 ASHE-ERIC Higher Education Reports

1. The Changing Nature of the Academic Deanship
   Mimi Wolverton, Walter H. Gmelch, Joni Montez, and Charles T. Nies

2. Faculty Compensation Systems: Impact on the Quality of Higher Education
   Terry P. Sutton, Peter J. Bergerson

3. Socialization of Graduate and Professional Students in Higher Education:
   A Perilous Passage?
   John C. Weidman, Darla J. Twale, Elizabeth Leahy Stein

4. Understanding and Facilitating Organizational Change in the 21st Century: Recent
   Research and Conceptualizations
   Adrianna J. Kezar

5. Cost Containment in Higher Education: Issues and Recommendations
   Walter A. Brown, Cayo Gamber

6. Facilitating Students' Collaborative Writing
   Bruce W. Speck

Back Issue/Subscription Order Form

Copy or detach and send to:
Jossey-Bass, A Wiley Company, 989 Market Street, San Francisco CA 94103-1741

Call or fax toll-free: Phone 888-378-2537 6:30AM — 3PM PST; Fax 888481-2665

Back Issues: Please send me the following issues at $24 each
(Important: please include series abbreviation and issue number. For example AEHE28:1)

_____

_____

_____

$ _____ Total for single issues

$ _____ SHIPPING CHARGES: SURFACE   Domestic Canadian
                                            First Item $5.00 $6.00
                                            Each Add I Item $3.00 $1.50
                       For next-day and second-day delivery rates, call the number listed above.

Subscriptions Please ❑ start ❑ renew my subscription to *ASHE-ERIC Higher Education Reports* for the year 2_____ at the following rate:

U.S.	❑ Individual $150	❑ Institutional $150
Canada	❑ Individual $150	❑ Institutional $230
All Others	❑ Individual $198	❑ Institutional $261
Online Subscription		❑ Institutional $150

**For more information about online subscriptions visit
www.interscience.wiley.com**

$ _____ Total single issues and subscriptions (Add appropriate sales tax for your state for single issue orders. No sales tax for U.S. subscriptions. Canadian residents, add GST for subscriptions and single issues.)

❑Payment enclosed (U.S. check or money order only)
❑VISA ❑ MC ❑ AmEx # _____ Exp. Date _____

Signature _____ Day Phone _____
❑ Bill Me (U.S. institutional orders only. Purchase order required.)

Purchase order # _____
                      Federal Tax ID13559302   **GST 89102 8052**

Name _____

Address _____

_____

Phone _____ E-mail _____

For more information about Jossey-Bass, visit our Web site at www.josseybass.com

PROMOTION CODE ND03

**ASHE-ERIC HIGHER EDUCATION REPORT
IS NOW AVAILABLE ONLINE AT WILEY INTERSCIENCE**

What is Wiley InterScience?

Wiley InterScience is the dynamic online content service from John Wiley & Sons delivering the full text of over 300 leading scientific, technical, medical, and professional journals, plus major reference works, the acclaimed Current Protocols laboratory manuals, and even the full text of select Wiley print books online.

What are some special features of Wiley InterScience?

Wiley Interscience Alerts is a service that delivers table of contents via e-mail for any journal available on Wiley InterScience as soon as a new issue is published online.
Early View is Wiley's exclusive service presenting individual articles online as soon as they are ready, even before the release of the compiled print issue. These articles are complete, peer-reviewed, and citable.
CrossRef is the innovative multi-publisher reference linking system enabling readers to move seamlessly from a reference in a journal article to the cited publication, typically located on a different server and published by a different publisher.

How can I access Wiley InterScience?

Visit http://www.interscience.wiley.com.

Guest Users can browse Wiley InterScience for unrestricted access to journal Tables of Contents and Article Abstracts, or use the powerful search engine.
Registered Users are provided with a *Personal Home Page* to store and manage customized alerts, searches, and links to favorite journals and articles. Additionally, Registered Users can view free Online Sample Issues and preview selected material from major reference works.
Licensed Customers are entitled to access full-text journal articles in PDF, with select journals also offering full-text HTML.

How do I become an Authorized User?

Authorized Users are individuals authorized by a paying Customer to have access to the journals in Wiley InterScience. For example, a University that subscribes to Wiley journals is considered to be the Customer.
Faculty, staff and students authorized by the University to have access to those journals in Wiley InterScience are Authorized Users. Users should contact their Library for information on which Wiley journals they have access to in Wiley InterScience.

ASK YOUR INSTITUTION ABOUT WILEY INTERSCIENCE TODAY!

Vasti Torres is an associate professor in the Higher Education and Student Affairs Program at Indiana University. She was previously a faculty member at The George Washington University. She received her doctorate in counseling and student affairs administration from the University of Georgia. Prior to becoming a faculty member she was associate vice provost and dean for enrollment and student services at Portland State University in Oregon. As an administrator she worked with freshman programs, academic advising, residence life and TRIO programs. She serves on the editorial board for the *Journal of College Student Development* and the *College Student Affairs Journal.* Her research interest focuses on the college experience of Latino students and Latino identity development. She was awarded a three-year Field Initiated Studies grant from the U.S. Department of Education to study the choice to stay in college for Latino students.

Mary F. Howard-Hamilton is associate professor and chair of the Higher Education and Student Affairs Program in the Department of Educational Leadership and Policy Studies at Indiana University. She received her Doctorate of Education from North Carolina State University and was a higher education administrator for fifteen years before becoming a faculty member, fulfilling duties including orientation, judicial affairs, multicultural affairs, commuter life, and residence life. As a faculty member, her areas of expertise are multicultural issues in higher education, student development theories, feminist theory and therapy, and consultation. As a researcher, she has published more than forty articles and book chapters. Her first book, *The Convergence of Race, Ethnicity, and Gender: Multiple Identities in Counseling,* was co-authored with Tracy Robinson. She also published *Student Services for Athletes* and is in the process of completing two additional books, *Diversity Issues in Higher Education* and *African American Women in Higher Education.*

Diane L. Cooper is an associate professor of college student affairs administration and department head of Counseling and Human Development Services at the University of Georgia. She received her Ph.D. from the University of Iowa in counselor education, with a concentration in postsecondary education and vocational development. She served for eight years as a student services practitioner in North Carolina before joining the faculty in student development at Appalachian State University. For six years she was the editor of the *College Student Affairs Journal* and on the editorial board for the *Journal of College Student Development* and the *Georgia Journal of College Student Affairs.* Her research interests are in program design and assessment, legal and ethical issues in student affairs practice, professional issues related to underrepresented groups in higher education, and improving staff development practices for all student services professionals.

Made in the USA
San Bernardino, CA
20 August 2015